I'M NOT
DOING IT
MYSELF

I'M NOT DOING IT MYSELF

The Comprehensive Guide to Managing a Home Construction or Renovation Project

HUGH HOWARD
for
Home Renovation Associates

FARRAR, STRAUS and GIROUX
NEW YORK

The architectural drawings in Chapter 2 are reproduced
courtesy of Loeffler, Johansen, Bennett, Architects, 821
Broadway, New York, New York 10003. The drawings and
design may be used only with written permission of the
architects.

Library of Congress Catalogue Card Number: 87-45091

*This book is dedicated to
John A. Howard, the man
who taught me tool sense.*

ACKNOWLEDGEMENTS

This book was made possible by the shared experience and training of numerous people. Home Renovation Associates would like to acknowledge the counsel of Richard Bennett, A.I.A., for his wise review of the manuscript and for the loan of his handsome design for the portfolio of plans; John P. Madden, whose engineering and law degrees and plain good sense lent guidance on many points; and David A. Thurm, who brought to bear not only his lawyerly training but also the experiences of one who has been there himself. All those kind enough to recollect their experiences are too numerous to mention here, but most prominent on the list are Robert Rice and Glenn Williams. Thanks, too, to Marjorie Anderson for her handsome design and John Gallagher for his help in developing the project.

Finally, I want to express my appreciation to Roger W. Straus III. The original idea for this book was his, and his reasoned and reasonable editorial guidance as it progressed made it better.

CONTENTS

I'M NOT DOING IT MYSELF

INTRODUCTION

The genesis of this book was a question: "How do you hire an architect?"

In a sense this book is an answer to that query. It is about deciding if an architect is needed, about finding the right one, then working well with him or her.

Yet *I'm Not Doing it Myself* is a good deal more than that, too. It goes beyond designing a new home or addition or remodeling job, and addresses the hiring, buying, borrowing, and other tasks involved in the actual construction process.

Note that I speak of building a new home and renovating an older one in the same breath. There is a reason for that. The process is the same for both, and this book is about managing that process, whether it involves the simple addition of a $500 deck or the construction of a $500,000 house.

One thing this book is not about, however, is how to do it yourself. There already exists a rich literature devoted to wielding tools and shaping materials. Some of those books are described at the end of this one (see "For Further Reading"). This book is about hiring the right pros to do the work for you and making sure they do it right.

I'm Not Doing it Myself is also about helping you avoid falling prey to the rip-offs and problems that are commonplace in the construction world. You've probably heard the classic story of the unscrupulous contractor who took the first payment and then disappeared for months. It has happened too many times to count, and one of the principal goals of this book is to tell you about such troubles so you won't be destined to repeat them.

Another of the classic situations to avoid is the one in which the contractor is really the inexperienced son of a friend who doesn't know what he is doing. The unsound structure he builds costs more to reconstruct a year later than it did to complete the first time around.

A less expensive but no less disquieting result is when every passerby can tell that no one with any design sense worked on your house. If you are one of those people who think they don't need an architect, perhaps you should look for the oddest-looking structure in the neighborhood. There's probably an independent-minded, who-needs-a-designer? kind of guy responsible for it.

There are traps out there, just waiting for the uninitiated to wander blithely into them. People frequently do. It is an everyday occurrence for people to pay for services they don't need, for markups they could have avoided, for talent that isn't as good as what is available for less. This book is designed to help you avoid such problems.

This book is also about saving you money. If you elect to be your own general contractor, you may save 20 percent or more of the total cost of your house. Chapter 3 is written specifically for the homeowner who is considering assuming the GC's role himself. If you find a stock plan that suits your needs, you may save the architect's fee, which often runs from 10 to 15 percent of the construction cost; in Chapter 2 we'll talk about stock plans. There are numerous other tips and suggestions for saving real dollars as you approach your construction project. Even if saving money is less important to you than getting exactly what you want, you will still find a great deal of guidance in these pages.

This book is full of advice. And there are statistics, architectural drawings, and lots of other useful information, data, and miscellaneous materials. But a key ingredient cannot be summarily reduced to numbers or even pictures.

Real-life dramas will be acted out on these pages. Talking about a place to live involves more than business facts and cold cash: a home is a place where emotions play a part, where instincts and an abstract sense of place are as important as dollars and cents. Personal tastes and feelings are crucially important as you think about your building project, whether it is that dream house you plan to inhabit for the rest of your life or the apartment you hope to resell in six months.

While *I'm Not Doing it Myself* is all about the business of construction, it also offers an understanding of the emotional steps in the process. They are inevitable—after all, it is a home space being created to individual tastes and specifications. A construction site normally has a disaster-like appearance, a fearsome sight that usually engenders feelings of frustration, inconvenience, and impatience with how long everything takes, especially if the residence is being lived in as the renovation is going on. Doubts about the process are inevitable; excitement, too, is natural, but often tempered by concerns of cost.

This book is intended to help you manage your home construction or renovation project. It aims to guide you in getting the most for your money, getting the job done on time, and getting what you want.

It's also about letting you in on what the experience is like. So why don't you join us in a tour of a few construction sites. Those of us who have been through it have learned a few things along the way, and the anecdotes in the Prologue that follows may help you prepare yourself for the adventure you are considering.

Hugh Howard
for
Home Renovation Associates

PROLOGUE

No renovation or construction project begins with the ringing of hammers and the screaming of Skil saws. In fact, the sounds of construction may well come rather late, often months or even years after conception.

The first event is most likely to be a quiet realization. It may be a small epiphany that comes to you as you try to squeeze one more piece of furniture into an already crammed space. It may be a realization that occurs after the joyous revelation that another child is on the way—and you know full well there just aren't enough bedrooms to go around. It may be a sad moment when you learn that your present home is about to be taken by eminent domain and you will have to start again someplace else. But whatever the cause, the impetus for this realization is usually plain, old-fashioned need.

The Planning Once you know a renovation or construction project is in your future, your next step is to try and quantify that need. You will have to decide for yourself what it is that you require.

In this context, buying construction services is much the same as buying groceries: you are more likely to end up satisfied with your purchases if you go into the store knowing roughly what you want. That beautiful steak may be the most appealing thing in the store, but it won't do you any good if your dinner guests are vegetarians. The same is true of house designs and building materials. Do your thinking and planning first; buy later.

I made a mistake of this kind on the first renovation project I undertook. My wife and I decided to renovate the kitchen in our large city apartment. It was a narrow, galley design, adjacent to a maid's room and half bath. No one who had lived in the apartment in the preceding thirty years had had a maid, and the maid's room and bath were too small to be of much use for anything but storage.

We summoned an architect friend. We gave him our priorities. We wanted a bigger kitchen and a utility room with washer and dryer. Needless to say, we wanted to spend as little money as possible. That was about as far as our thoughts had taken us.

He asked us a lot of questions. In retrospect, I'm afraid we gave him a lot of vague, poorly considered answers. So he looked around carefully, measured the spaces, and went away.

He came back with a perspective drawing of a kitchen relocated into what had been the maid's room and bath, which together offered us the bigger space we wanted. The old kitchen was to be converted to the utility room. The whole design seemed just right, and required a minimum of renovation (and, therefore, expense). The drawing won our approval immediately, and we asked the architect to go to final plans. My wife and I patted one another on the back, confident that we had the home renovation game all figured out.

The demolition to open up the space that was to be the new kitchen began shortly afterward. As the walls came down, we saw a larger, more appealing space. The old kitchen and maid's room and bath were one and, suddenly, we knew we wanted more. We saw a full-fledged eat-in kitchen, more windows with morning light and good views. The separate kitchen and utility room just didn't make sense to us anymore. So it was back to the drawing board.

In the end, we did get exactly what we wanted (that is, we got what we finally realized we wanted). We were thrilled with the finished product. But it did cost us twice as much as we had budgeted: the architect had to do his job twice (he had executed final plans by the time we changed our minds) and it was a bigger job than he had originally specified. And it took almost twice as long, too, as the schedule got completely out of sync when we changed our minds.

What would we do differently if we were starting today? We would establish what we wanted earlier rather than later. In order to help others make up their minds sooner, we've set out a questionnaire in Chapter 1. It is intended to help you formulate as specifically as possible what it is you want. So you don't have to do any of it twice.

Let's suppose that you have gotten to the stage where you know what you want in terms of approximate size and number of rooms. That's the time to hire an architect/designer and/ or contractor to design and build it for you. It isn't always easy, as the experience of Denise and David suggests.

Their home was a converted squash court on what had been a large estate on the so-called Gold Coast of Long Island, New York. The house had a spectacular living room with hardwood plank walls that extended almost twenty-five feet up to a cathedral ceiling and enormous skylight. There was a monumental Victorian spiral staircase from a defunct bank in Maine, and a view of the water worth writing home about. The lone drawback was that the rest of the house consisted of a narrow TV room, a smallish kitchen, and a comfortable but hardly enormous bedroom.

In short, they owned a piece of property with million-dollar potential but such severe space limitations that it was hard to entertain weekend guests, not to mention raising the children they were considering bringing into the world.

Denise and David knew they wanted the addition to respect the architectural integrity of the building they were expanding. They knew approximately how much addition space and how many rooms they wanted. And their budget, while not unlimited, was generous. In short, theirs was the kind of job most architects love: an aesthetic challenge with a good deal of freedom.

They knew from day one that an addition was in their future, so almost before they got the coffee water boiling on the stove they began thinking and looking and talking new space. Neither of them had formal design training or construction experience, so they decided to talk to an expert. They made an appointment for a consultation at the architectural firm of Robert A. M. Stern.

Stern is probably the most visible residential architect of our day. His television series on architecture, *Pride of Place,* ran on the Public Broadcasting System in 1986. He has published books on architecture, and his designs are much discussed and admired.

David and Denise arrived at his Manhattan offices armed with photographs of their house, a site plan, and great expectations, but no fixed idea of what they wanted. They met with an associate of the firm. They were told that for $10,000 the firm would be most pleased to design an addition for them and execute a model for their consideration. Final working plans and construction supervision would be additional expenses.

If the fee seems high, look at it this way: the construction cost would be in the neighborhood of a quarter of a million dollars. However, at that point David and Denise were looking for someone who would brainstorm with them, who would try to understand their needs, an architect who would work with them, not one who would deliver a fait accompli. Denise sells and collects art and prides herself on having an instinct for color and form; David is a practical person and was quite conscious of the fact that he was going to be watching TV and bringing up his children in that place, and he wanted it to suit his needs and tastes. Needless to say, the firm of Stern did not get that commission.

The next try was no more successful. An interior designer came knocking on David and Denise's door one rainy Sunday afternoon. He was a friend of a friend, had heard they were considering adding on, and came to offer his services. He had never done a design job of the magnitude of Denise and David's, but he was eager to take on the challenge. He was a rising star on the interior design scene in New York City, and he offered to do a first set of renderings, complete with elevations and floor plans, at no charge. If Denise and David liked them, they would negotiate a mutually acceptable fee for the whole job; if they didn't, then it was his loss, not theirs.

The three of them sat down and debriefed one another. The designer then disappeared to his drawing board, and Denise and David were left to await the results of their conversation.

When the designer returned, they were shocked at what he had drawn. It was nearly half again the size (and therefore the cost) of what they had asked for. It totally transformed the old façade (which they had told him they wanted to retain) by adding a new central section flanked by the original building on one side and a new mirror image of the old on the other. So much for that attempt.

Next David called an old high school friend who had become a licensed architect. His were primarily commercial designs, but he thought the job sounded like a good change of pace. He came over and looked.

As is usual with such meetings, the homeowners talked at length with the architect. He tried to elicit from them as much hard information about expectations and needs as possible; they tried to describe to him the shape and feel and impression of their dream.

As an architect who specialized in office installations, he had a computer that drew floor plans. He would feed in specifications and out would come the plans; he could change a few specs and new plans would appear from the computer's printer.

They had several more meetings, each of which involved reviewing a gradually evolving floor plan. The three of them seemed to be getting closer to the right layout, but Denise and David weren't quite satisfied. Perhaps the architect sensed this, because one day he called and said he just didn't have time to continue with the process. He was having trouble keeping up with his commercial work, he said. He didn't have to say that the other work was also a great deal more profitable. So sorry, he concluded, I can't help you now, but maybe next year?

They then talked to another nationally known architect, who told them he wouldn't work for a penny less than 15 percent of construction cost and that he thought the budget should be more like $400,000 than $250,000. Needless to say, they have yet to break ground for their addition. "Probably next spring," David says. But at present, they have no plan—or architect.

There is often an immense difference between what you see in your mind's eye and what your designer actually puts on paper, as David and Denise learned. Even when the architect does put on paper what you want, it may not be the answer. You may not express yourself clearly (after all, few of us have formal design training or even an instinct for talking articulately about shapes and styles and spatial relationships). The architect/designer may not elicit key information from you as well as he should. And both of you may be guilty of not listening to the other. It just goes to show how important it is to work at communicating clearly with your designer: the paper realization of your dream is all-important, so make sure you're all talking the same language.

The more carefully you plan, the better off you (and your wallet) will be when it comes to the construction. Denise and David haven't gotten their addition underway yet—but they also haven't rushed ahead and commissioned a halfway satisfactory structure just for the sake of getting it done. Don't be in a hurry early or you'll regret it later.

The Construction Now, suppose you love the plans, they fit your needs and your tastes, the budget work is done and you have your financing. You have a builder ready to go to work. What's next?

Chaos is one word that comes to mind. It comes to lots of people's minds who try to live within a construction project. Even if you don't, steel yourself for the chaos.

The story of Scott and Deborah, an Oregon couple, is instructive. They planned a major renovation job for a time when they would be on vacation for four weeks. They figured that it would be perfect: they were taking the kids and dogs, they wouldn't have to live with the plaster dust, and the builder assured them it was "a piece of cake" to finish the job in the time allotted.

Not every job lends itself to such in absentia treatment, but in this case there were few decisions to make and Scott's brother lived next door, so he could inspect the work daily while they were away. And the brother was more comfortable with tools anyway, so it all made sense. They booked the builder's time in advance, worked out a delivery schedule for the materials, and went off for Southern California.

So what went wrong? Ironically, nothing did. The builder met his schedule, the materials all arrived, and he did a fine job, thanks in part to the brother's attentive inspections. There was only one little problem: Scott and Deb came home a day early. And they found their house in the most unholy mess imaginable. Fragile furniture was piled on top of fragile furniture and a layer of dust the thickness of a wet spring snowfall coated everything. The rugs were filthy, the yard was cluttered with wood scraps and shingle fragments and tools and enough obstacles to dispatch any careless adult—not to mention toddler son, Scott Jr.—to the emergency room. Deb had an almost irresistible desire to attack the builder bodily for destroying her home.

But the builder volunteered to pay for a night in a hotel. He told them not to come back until after three o'clock the next afternoon, by which time the cleaning firm he had contracted to clean the place would have come and gone.

To Scott and Deb's amazement, a short twenty-four hours later they returned to a house at least as clean as the one they had left a month earlier. But the shock of seeing their house in an apparent shambles stays with them.

Construction sites are more than messy. They can also be dangerous. On the other hand, perhaps the greatest source of delight in experiencing the renovation or construction process firsthand is the opportunity to see a structure emerge from a disparate array of materials. Most architects and designers admit to a sense of wonder about it all—and the honest ones even admit that while much of the finished product was clearly envisioned on the drawing, some of it was not. The experience may even provide you with a better sense of how to enjoy your home.

The case of Eli and Jane's old barn in Virginia suggests this potential for discovery. They knew full well even before they began that by opening windows in the barn walls they would make it a lighter, more open building. But what they didn't anticipate was the effect they would get in the hayloft that was to be converted to the master bedroom.

To everyone's surprise, when the barn was cleaned out, the loft was found to have interior walls of old, rich cedar. Instead of hanging a drywall and plaster surface on the walls, as the original plans had called for, they decided to salvage the cedar. The architect had already suggested a couple of skylights, so the parts all seemed to be coming together.

One of Jane's recollections summarizes the pleasure of the experience for them. Jane and Eli had come to visit the work site on a Saturday afternoon. There were no workmen to interfere or be interfered with, so they had the place to themselves. The job was by no means finished, but the skylights were in place and the cedar adorned the walls of the converted loft. Little or no finish work had been done, but the basic shape of the place was there.

They walked around and looked at what had been done since their last visit, upstairs and down. They made notes about this and that in order to discuss them with the architect and builders. Then they decided to go home.

Jane went out to the car. When Eli didn't arrive in a few minutes, she went back to look for him, a little worried that he might have hurt himself. Eli, a disciplined man who always does what he says he's going to do and arrives when he says he is going to, was found sitting on the floor in the new master bedroom. He was watching the warm, quiet red light of the setting sun play on the wall. As Jane says, "I'd never seen him sit still and do nothing before. I knew then that we'd done the right thing."

As Jane and Eli's experience suggests, if you begin with good planning and yet remain flexible and open to change when opportunity knocks, there are often happy surprises to be uncovered and taken advantage of.

There are moments of irritation, too, in any construction project. Every job seems to take longer than it should. Sometimes progress seems to stop for days or even weeks at a time. In renovation work, days can disappear while the work of correcting this or that unforeseen problem is done. Renovation work is always a great adventure: no matter how experienced your professional help is, they are unlikely to know exactly what opening the walls or floors or ceilings will reveal; usually, there's good news and bad.

At times the progress in new construction also can seem to come to a dead stop. While the plumbers and electricians are roughing in their pipes and wires, visible progress may seem at a standstill. A delay or scheduling conflict may mean that at times literally nothing does get done for a while, but that's where good scheduling comes in.

One almost universal joke in the construction business is the old line "It'll be done in a couple of weeks." The words can be said seriously or while smiling. "It'll be done in a couple of weeks" can be a real answer (only rarely) or a way of saying, "Hey, get off my back, will you? I got work to do here." In more than one rehab project I can recall, the words "It'll be done in a couple of weeks" were heard every week for several months.

The Completion No building or renovation project goes like clockwork, no matter how much care and experience are invested. There are problems and holdups and changes and disagreements and mistakes and redos. In a sense, the situation is akin to what every coach concerned with conditioning his athletes has said a thousand times: if it doesn't hurt, it isn't doing you any good. A construction or renovation project shouldn't, of course, be painful, but if there aren't moments of disagreement and difficulty, then you're living in a more perfect world than I live in. Or you are accepting things uncritically.

One classic completion story is the one about the home renovator who decided he wanted to do a small portion of the work himself. It wasn't so much to save money as it was to feel more a part of the whole process. He arranged with the contractor to hang the drywall in his new dining area but to leave it unfinished: John would apply the tape and joint compound and finish the job himself.

Which he did. And even today, several years later, he will proudly point to the portion of the job he did himself and describe the role he played. But what he doesn't recall for his visitors (though his wife invariably does) is that he finished his portion of the work more than three weeks after the contractor completed the rest. So for nearly a month after everything else was painted and clean, they had to live with gypsum dust and paint smells and the rest.

This book is about getting the job finished: dreaming it up, getting it designed, getting it built and then finished. There is a great thrill to the moment when the bills are paid and the tools have been moved out and the punch list of last-minute fixes and details has been taken care of. That identifiable moment of completion is the biggest argument there is for hiring people to do a job for you rather than trying to take it on yourself.

This book is concerned with home space, about the construction and renovation of places where people live and love. That makes it a book about the very personal business of home construction. Yet at the same time, it is very much about the professional problems of that same process, about dollars and contracts and negotiations and arbitrations and insurance and the rest.

So let us get to the business at hand, and start thinking about *your* home.

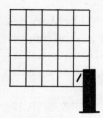

1

VISIONS

Deciding What You Want

Exactly what is it that you want to do?

This chapter will help you decide for yourself what you want; the chapters that follow will help you get it done.

We are concerned with two kinds of home construction. One is new construction, the from-nothing creation of an entirely new house or an addition to an existing home. The second kind is remodeling: you may be finishing the unfinished, converting a basement or attic into a livable, finished space; or you may be changing what you already have in your home or apartment.

Building a new house is not the same as, say, putting a second bath in that small back bedroom, but the steps in the process are essentially the same. The bigger the project, the more time, money, and headaches are involved, but it is generally a matter of more of the same elements.

Regardless of the scope of your project, the first step is to decide what you want and need.

Establishing your NEEDS is likely to be simple, and the questionnaire that begins below can help you determine quite specifically what it is you need: the number of rooms, the size each should be, and so on.

The harder part is determining what it is you want. While need has to do with quantitative determinations like the number of bedrooms required for your family, wants and wishes are much more subjective. As a first step toward actual construction, you'll have to create—and or have created—plans that conform to the requirements of local building ordinances. So as a first step toward those plans, you need to make numerous subjective decisions about style and materials and answer a multitude of questions for yourself or your architect/designer.

Complete the questionnaire that follows so that you will have a firm grasp on what it is you need. You may be surprised at how little or how much space you require. Armed with the hard information from the questionnaire, go on to the next section. It will help you develop some sense of a design you can live with.

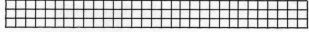

QUESTIONNAIRE

Why go to the trouble of filling out a questionnaire?

Years ago I heard this story from an architect friend. A new client had hired him to design a house for her. She knew pretty much what she wanted; she needed so many bedrooms, and wanted to use the site in such and such a way. She had a fondness for a certain architectural style, but the most important of her predilections was her concern for some family heirlooms. She wanted a suitable space for them.

My architect friend did some preliminary sketches for her of floor plans and an elevation. He designed the house around a central

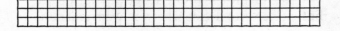

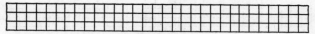

staircase/foyer/gallery space that gave the antique furniture and paintings a suitable space for display (some of the objects were large and needed the reach of the two-story space). He also met her budget and other requirements.

She liked what she saw, and after a small amount of discussion and a few changes, she told him to proceed to working drawings. She approved of those, too, and they engaged a contractor.

The construction went without a hitch. Until at three o'clock one morning our architect friend got a call from his client.

"It won't fit!" She was hysterical.

"What won't fit?"

"My tall clock!"

He was confused. Even though it was the middle of the night, he was thinking clearly and he was sure she hadn't mentioned a tall clock among her antiques. Not only that, but she had been to the site the previous evening, and they had walked through the building. It wasn't finished, but the roof was on and the windows in, so for the first time it was possible to walk around the place and get a sense of its shape and configuration.

They talked. He learned that her mother had long before promised her another very valuable family heirloom to add to her collection. It was a grandfather clock, complete with brass works, that had been in the family since the time of the Revolution. Her mother was still alive and well and living a few miles away, the tall clock with her, but the daughter held a vivid image in her mind's eye of that clock on the stairway landing of her beautiful new foyer. The problem was, she had never told her architect, and even the most experienced architect can't be expected to be a mind reader.

So go through the questionnaire that

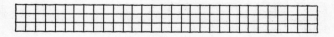

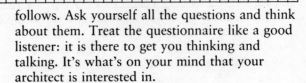

follows. Ask yourself all the questions and think about them. Treat the questionnaire like a good listener: it is there to get you thinking and talking. It's what's on your mind that your architect is interested in.

Don't go through this questionnaire as if it were a standardized examination to which there are right answers. The point is for you to consider some key issues and, in turn, to get your feelings and desires across to your architect. And they shouldn't be only the feelings of one member of your family: if you all have to live there, get everybody involved.

What happened to the lady and her tall clock? It wasn't too late to make a couple of small changes in the layout of the second floor, although it was expensive.

THE LOCATION

The underlying assumption of this book is that you already own the house or apartment you plan to renovate or the piece of land on which you plan to build. So in that sense, location is not at issue here.

However, location does affect many other decisions.

One value judgment you should make before proceeding is whether you are talking about building a new home or improving an existing one right out of the marketplace. That's always a bad idea. Make sure you know the real estate values in your neighborhood before proceeding.

THE SITE: Unless your job involves only remodeling or finishing off interior space, your architect will need a site plan. A survey probably was done at the time you bought the property, but if no survey exists, you may have to arrange for a surveyor to conduct one or pay your architect an additional fee to do his own site inspection. Ideally, you should also provide him with a topographical map of the property.

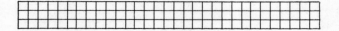

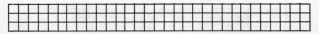

Do you have any specific feelings about the terrain and how the house should be situated on the property?

ORIENTATION: Do you want the façade of the house to face the street or not? Is there a vista that you want to take special advantage of? What about the sun? Many successful designs try to locate the kitchen so that it receives east (morning) light, and dining or relaxation areas to take advantage of afternoon sun. If no one in your household cares about a sunny breakfast space, then perhaps it makes more sense to make that the office area.

Obviously, your concern with light is influenced by your climate: if you live amid snow and brutal cold much of the year, the more sun the better, while in a tropical or subtropical area you want to minimize the effects of the sun's rays.

Do you want your building to be oriented in a particular direction?

Which rooms do you want facing in which directions?

Are there views you want to incorporate into your design, window, or deck arrangements?

ZONING, SETBACKS, ETC.: What dictates are there in the neighborhood? What limitations are you faced with on your deed? You must provide your architect with specifics as to setback and rights-of-way so he can work around them.

If there are such limitations, what are they?

THE SIZE

OVERALL SIZE: How big a house do you need?
How many bedrooms?   1   2   3
More:
Is a family room essential?   Yes   No
Separate dining room?   Yes   No
Eat-in kitchen?   Yes   No

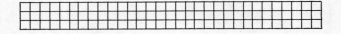

ROOM SIZE: What are your square-foot space needs?

Room	Dimension	Square Feet
Entry/vestibule area	___ × ___	___
Living room	___ × ___	___
Kitchen	___ × ___	___
Dining room	___ × ___	___
TV/family room	___ × ___	___
Master bedroom	___ × ___	___
Bedroom	___ × ___	___
Bedroom	___ × ___	___
Bathrooms	___ × ___	___
Office/den	___ × ___	___

Space desired: _____ square feet

Add 20% for halls, _____ square feet
walls, closets, stairs,
etc.:

TOTAL SPACE: _____ SQUARE FEET

THE DESIGN

THE STYLE:
Attach a photograph and in a few sentences describe the style of the house or addition you want.
How many stories?
1 __ 1½ __ 2 __ 2½ __
Is the project an addition to an existing home?
Are you finishing off an unfinished space in your present home?

THE EXTERIOR:
Exterior material: Wood, stone, brick, aluminum or vinyl siding?
Windows: What kind? Double-hung, casement, awning, sliding, skylights?

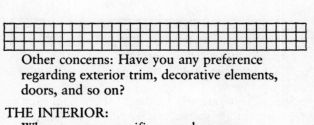

Other concerns: Have you any preference regarding exterior trim, decorative elements, doors, and so on?

THE INTERIOR:

What are your specific room-by-room requirements?

ENTRY/VESTIBULE AREA: Closet required?
Table, chairs, other furniture to be planned for?
Size of furniture?
Floor covering?
Special wall or ceiling surfaces? (Most new interior surfaces today are of drywall construction; specify if you want wood paneling or other finish.)
Special considerations: Lighting? Windows? Doors?
Other entrances necessary? (E.g., from mudroom, garage, or cellar?)

KITCHEN: Special lighting considerations?
Floor covering?
Special wall or ceiling surfaces?
Washer/dryer to be located in kitchen?
Eating space? If so, for how many?
Visual access to dining or living areas?

DINING ROOM: Is a separate dining room necessary?
Furniture to be planned around?
Floor covering?
Special wall or ceiling surfaces?
Seating for how many at table required?

LIVING ROOM: Sofa, chairs, rugs, artwork, or other furniture or decorative elements to be planned for?
Floor covering?
Special wall or ceiling surfaces?
Fireplace?
What activities do you anticipate this room will be used for?
Do you entertain often? If so, how many people must you allow for?
Closet requirements?

TV/FAMILY ROOM: Floor covering?

Special wall or ceiling surfaces?
What activities do you anticipate this room will be used for?
Special furniture requirements? (E.g., pool table, projection TV screen, etc.?)
Closet requirements?
Bar?

MASTER BEDROOM: Private bath?
Separate dressing room?
Special sound-proofing necessary?
Floor covering?
Closet requirements?
Special wall or ceiling surfaces?

CHILDREN'S BEDROOMS: How many?
Closet requirements?
Floor covering?
Special wall or ceiling surfaces?

GUEST BEDROOM: Closet requirements?
Floor covering?
Special wall or ceiling surfaces?
Will this room be used for family activities as well? Hobbies, work, study?

BATHROOMS: How many? Where located(floor, within master bedroom, adjacent to kitchen, etc.)
Bathtub or shower?
Closet requirements?
Linen closet?
Bidet?
Half-bath? Where located?
Floor covering?
Special wall or ceiling surfaces?

OFFICE/DEN: Desk?
Chairs?
Closet requirements?
Other furniture?
Filing cabinet?
Bookshelves?
Floor covering?
Special wall or ceiling surfaces?

UTILITY ROOM: What will the space contain?

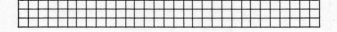

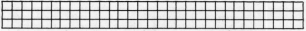

HVAC (heating, ventilation, air conditioning) equipment? Washer and dryer? Hot-water heater?
Closet requirements?

OTHER ROOMS: Darkroom?
Special storage area?

OTHER SPACES: Basement? Workshop, storage, etc.?
Garage?
Deck?
Greenhouse?
Wine cellar?
Stable, shed, other outbuildings?

ROOM RELATIONSHIPS:
Are there some rooms that you would group together, others you would separate? E.g., would you put the master bedroom at one end of the house and the children's room at the other? The nursery adjacent? Would you put the living room away from the master bedroom? And so on. List your priorities.

OTHER CONSIDERATIONS

MECHANICAL NEEDS:
Air conditioning?
Zoned heating?
Other special considerations?

SPECIAL CONCERNS:
Should you be anticipating a considerable change in the usual patterns of your home? For example, will some or all of your children shortly be leaving the nest? Are you expecting another one? What about an elderly parent coming to live with you?
If you are remodeling, is your present house energy-inefficient, and should you be considering retrofitting it with insulation or another heat source, etc.?
Have you considered all of your special needs in specifying your rooms? Keep in mind such issues as privacy, the individual hobbies practiced by members of the household, any contradictory

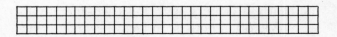

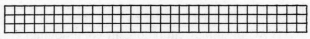

schedules of household members, lighting needs, noise factors, and so on.

THE COST:
How much can you spend?

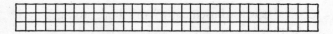

Exploring the Possibilities

Think about the project from several different standpoints. One is context: you're not living in a vacuum, so you must regard your house as being part of a larger picture. Another key issue is style, with the related matters of shape and form. By considering these broad issues and others, perhaps you can inform your thinking about wishes and wants.

What's the Context? Unless you're building on the moon, there is an architectural context. In adding on to an existing house, the context is obvious. The shape and style and configuration of what you are starting with constitute the principal context.

If your project is a new house, the context is the other houses nearby. Even if the property is isolated and the house will not be seen in conjunction with any others, regional styles and influences still remain. Think about it this way: even in a totally isolated setting, a New England saltbox is still a jarring sight in arid Arizona; in the same way, a solo California rancho-style home looks peculiar indeed on the Canadian border in a snowstorm.

Context is determined by many factors, including the site or plot, the immediate neighborhood and the broader community, and the environment within which it is located.

Consider this situation. In a small town in upstate New York, Main Street has been lined for nearly a century with tall (two-and-a-half-story) Victorian houses. In fact, the street is virtually an essay on the diversity of Victorian styling, with Carpenter Gothic, Queen Anne, Second Empire, and other styles represented. The houses, though virtually all different, are very much of a piece: they look like siblings even with all the years that have passed since their construction and the innumerable alterations, large and small, made in those intervening years.

A contributing element in the continuity of this pleasantly diverse collection of houses is the alignment of their façades with one another. The setback from the street is consistent, no doubt established by prudence and good sense rather than statute.

Suddenly, in the fall of 1985, a new house appeared amid the row. It was a log house, built in the front yard of one of the Victorian houses.

The effect was devastating: sitting forward of all the other houses, the log house became the first building to catch the eye. The tidy line of Victorians was diminished to a secondary role. Not only is the log house the first focus when driving by, but it looks very much out of place among the other houses. It appears to be a well-built and commodious home, but it is grotesquely out of context.

This is an extreme example of a house that violates the unwritten understanding that neighborhoods often seem to evolve. But it does suggest the kind of thinking about style and plot positioning that you need to do before building.

In the last twenty-odd years, a strong movement has emerged to preserve our architectural past. There are pros and cons about which experts argue, but the fact is that there is now a respect—in some cases, even a reverence— for America's architectural heritage.

If you are renovating an older home or if your new home is in a historic district, you may confront a miscellany of rules and regulations; we'll talk about those in the next section of this chapter. But the presence of "old" in your home adds another aspect to "context."

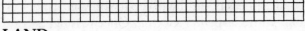

LAND

This book isn't about buying land; the assumption here is that you know where you want to build your new home or that you are adding to an older one. Many publications are available to help you know what's best in buying land, but they seem to say the same things in different, longer-winded ways. So our advice here is threefold:

1. "Three factors determine the value of a piece of real estate," asserts the old cliché. "Location, location, and location." You may be tired of hearing it, but remember it because it's true.

2. The second advisory is a corollary to the first: Whether you are renovating or building, keep in mind that the potential value of your home is limited by the potential of its location. To put it another way, if you construct a $250,000 house in a neighborhood of $100,000 homes, don't expect to be able to sell it for a profit in the short term. Location is, again, a limiting factor. Conversely, then, it is always a good idea to improve on a house that is less valuable than most of its neighbors.

3. If you are buying property, be sure that your attorney incorporates into the contract a clause to protect you in the event the land is incapable of bearing the weight of your house (some soils will not) or if for any other reason you cannot build on it (inadequate drainage, zoning requirements, no potable water, etc.).

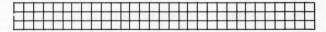

A brief vocabulary lesson is in order. The set of words that apply here are often used interchangeably by the layman, but within the strict confines of architectural historic preservation, they mean very different things.

George Stephen, author of *Remodeling*

Old Houses (see "For Further Reading," page 174), carefully distinguishes between restoration, rehabilitation (rehab), and redesign. Restoration involves returning a structure to its "original" appearance. Often much detective work must be done to determine what is truly original and what is not; a purist restorer will go so far as to remove whole wings of a house that were added after its original construction.

Rehabilitation is a simpler process. A building that has been rehabilitated is one that has been made habitable once again. There may be some reorganization of what came before, but generally the basic design will not be changed in a rehabilitation. In redesign, radical changes are made, perhaps obliterating any similarity to the original structure.

One reason the meanings of these words have blurred is that in the case of a restoration, for example, it is impossible truly to restore it to its "original" condition. No one can really know what that Cape was like when its colonial inhabitants lived in it and, besides, who wants to live without running water and electricity in this age? Nevertheless, in dealing with an older home—or even with a new house in an area in which older homes predominate—you should be conscious of what came before.

Context is more than a matter of what the houses around yours look like or even how yours began its existence. There are a number of other key questions that you must consider about your site. For instance, do you want to use or avoid the sun's heat? In cooler climates, you'll want to harness as much of the sun's cold-weather heat as possible, while in warmer climes you are likely to take pains to shield the house's interior as much as possible from direct solar effects. In the same way, you must consider other elements: what of the wind on that high hill? Perhaps you should build just below the peak and be content with the vistas on one side rather than insist on multiple exposures. What about the runoff from a rain or snowmelt in your favorite spot in that little valley next to the stream?

Another site issue is privacy. How will you locate the house in general and each of its sides vis-à-vis the street?

If your project is the remodeling of an apartment, then your primary contextual concern is the portions of the apartment you are not redoing. Will you be creating two jarringly different environments? You may also wish to consider other apartments and the public spaces in the building: guests emerging from a stately old elevator to enter your ultramodern apartment may find the contrast disturbing.

Whatever your project, be sure to consider whether your notions work with the environment or against it.

What's the Style? Robert Frost once said that writing free verse (poetry without rhyme or meter) was rather like playing tennis without a net. It can be done, of course, but it's done better by those who know how to play with the net first, so that when they go off and free-form, they understand the basic disciplines and rituals of the game.

Making architectural choices about your house is much the same: if you know something of the rules and rituals other people have played by, you at least know which of them you are flouting. Your decisions can then be conscious and considered, and the chances that you will second-guess yourself later will be much reduced.

Perhaps the single most important issue in thinking about a house design, whatever its context, is its style.

Let's not abandon context entirely, however, as local or neighboring architectural styles are important factors. Remember our log house amid the Victorians. That house might well be generally acknowledged as stylish in the woods but it's certainly an oddity on Main Street.

One dictionary definition of style is "a manner or mode of writing." Just as a writing style is characterized by the use of certain words in a certain way, architectural styles are identified by their use of certain materials and methods. So identifying established styles is relatively easy: there are handbooks that will help you distinguish one style from another. If you don't know exactly what you want and are interested in fixing your tastes within a historical perspective, you will find that a stylebook will help. (One architectural stylebook, *What Style Is It?*, published by the Preservation Press in conjunction with the U.S. Department of the Interior, is a particularly accessible introduction. See "For Further Reading.")

It seems that houses come in more styles than colors. Traditional colonial styles alone can be divided into four basic types on the basis of national origin, as English-, Spanish-, Dutch-, and French-influenced designs are distinctively different. The early American and Victorian periods offer even more variations, while the twentieth century has added its share of innovations with the bungalow, ranch, split-level, and the rest.

Today, architects are reacting against the modernist ethos that in recent decades has seemed to demand that traditional style be abandoned for new designs. Now a new vocabulary is evolving, in which architects draw on elements of our architectural heritage and integrate them with modern sensibilities. Traditional columns, so popular in Georgian and Greek Revival styles, have reappeared. The simplicity, the plainness of the modern industrial style is giving way to—or melding with—elements of other areas. As one New England architect, Peter Gluck, puts it: "Now it's allowable, acceptable even, for there to be a dialogue between modernism and history."

While the identifying aspects of various styles can be learned from a book, trying to establish workable parameters for what is "stylish" is a little like trying to catch a unicorn: it's a wonderful exercise of the imagination but somehow no one seems to be able to do it. The rules keep changing as tastes change. If you don't know exactly what you want, learn a little bit about styles, and establish what it is you like. Find houses that are attractive to your eye, and determine what style they are. When it comes time to convey to your architect and/or builder what it is you are looking for, a specific knowledge of your choice of style, complete with illustrations of it, is an important aspect in getting what you want. To his trained eye, a simple snapshot will go far to identify your tastes.

SHAPE AND FORM. Style is determined by a number of factors: ornamentation and materials are important, but the shape and form suggest a great deal about a house. It is the roofline and the shape and relationship of the walls that determine the overall form and mass of the home.

The first question is: what is its basic shape? Is it a square or a pyramid? Is it shaped like a shoe box or a silo? Is it some combination of geometric shapes?

The second question is: how are the openings positioned? Are the doors and windows all in a row, or is there a calculatedly (accidental?) randomness?

What is the texture and pattern of the siding and trim? Are the clapboards all lines in a row? Is there an elaborately carved cornice? Is there lots of trim or is barrenness the rule?

In order to help you think about the house you are building or renovating, here are the common basic configurations you are likely to choose from.

The One-Story House. The standard ranch is perhaps the best example of the one-story house. It is also the most frequently constructed configuration. Its advantages include no stairs to climb and inexpensive construction costs; also, it is the easiest to maintain, as there is less climbing of ladders and scaffolding involved with painting and roofing and other tasks.

The One-and-a-Half-Story House. These days, fewer and fewer houses of this compromise design are built. While it does have a second floor, the side walls are not of full height, so the upstairs ceilings pitch downward. It is a proven design, however, as the Pilgrims set up housekeeping quite successfully in their Cape Cod one-and-a-half-story designs.

The good news about the one-and-a-half-story arrangement is that a second floor is to be had for next to nothing in terms of building materials and costs. The bad news is that the saving is rarely passed on to the consumer; and to some it doesn't seem like much of a bargain, given the built-in limitations on ventilation, light, and headroom on the second floor.

The Two-Story House. This is perhaps the classic American family home: can you imagine any of the television sitcoms of the early sixties without banisters for the children to slide down on and upstairs bedrooms to banish them to?

It is an efficient design, as, in a sense, it uses one foundation twice and is easy to heat. But there are stairs to climb, a hardship for some.

The Split-Level. The split-level has compromise written all over it. It draws upon the other designs, in particular the two-story house, but is distinct in that its entry is at a level in between the first and second floors, in a sense "splitting" the house.

The split-level can be constructed on a small lot, like the two-story house. It will take up a minimum of space while providing a maximum of interior living area.

Areas of the house can be isolated from the rest, which can be an advantage. But a house of this design is difficult to heat, and many people find having living areas on the first floor unsatisfactory, as it often feels as if they are underground.

Remodeling Notes: A Note on the Exterior

The logical approach to thinking about a home is to begin with the inside. You will spend most of your time there, so it should be your first priority. That's why architects usually start with floor and flow plans.

If, however, you are adding on to an existing house, you must consider that what goes on inside affects the outside, too. That new door you want to add may unbalance a calculatedly symmetrical façade. That new wing you are thinking of adding to the side of your house will affect what you see out front; if you decide you want windows larger than those of the rest of the house, consider how they will look outside— are they all out of sync with what came before?

One house I inspected for a friend some years ago started life as a captain's house in the eighteenth century. The rooms are small, in keeping with the scale of the people and the heating facilities and the lifestyle of pre-revolutionary America. However, its present owner had added a grand room of classical proportions. It has a handsome coffin ceiling, elaborate moldings, and elegant French doors that look out onto Long Island Sound. The room is almost palatial. But the house looks like a Model T grafted to a Rolls-Royce.

A simple and sensible rule of thumb is to try to remain consistent with the existing house. But if you don't have to go to architecture school to sense that, then why do so many people ignore it? If for some reason it is not possible to respect what is there and you choose to go off in another stylistic direction, have the courage of your convictions and do it. That is, don't make some halfhearted compromises and end up with a house that has no discernible style and looks like what it is, an unsuccessful marriage.

Two of the most critical elements in any addition are the roof and the windows. The configuration, slope, and overhang of the roof are the key elements; window style and position are also important. Once again, try to match them up or, failing that, try to create a dialogue between the old and the new that says something to the observer instead of merely appearing to be in the middle of a pointless argument.

Another important element is the siding. Generally new siding is easy to match up with old, and it provides much of the texture of any house. You can use siding to unify or to contrast.

The bottom line is that in adding on to any house with a distinct style, you either use that style or you lose it.

Interior Layout You may have a great variety of criteria you wish to apply to the house. If you have a drummer in your family, you may need a soundproof room in an isolated corner of the house for use as a music room. If a member of your family is confined to a wheelchair, you may require ramp access to the house and between levels inside. You know your concerns better than anyone else, so make sure you have them in mind—and that you make them clear to your architect—as you go about the planning process.

Consider how the proportions of each room affect its use. Is your dining room, for example, very long, so that there is wasted space at one end while the table area is cramped? One very common room shape is a rectangle about twice as long as it is wide. Are there corners that are useless or ceilings that are too low or exaggeratedly high?

Most effective designs divide a house into three main areas: the private or bedroom area, the work area (including the kitchen and utility room), and the relaxation area. The latter generally includes the living and dining rooms, sometimes a recreation or family room as well.

The layout of your new or renovated space should make allowances for the different uses of the various areas and their interrelationship. For example, the relaxation area is probably not well located if it is immediately below the nursery; if it is, you're almost sure to disturb your sleeping baby when you entertain. In the same way, is your den or office area out of the major traffic lanes or will your concentration be forever interrupted by everyone who comes and goes? Is there a secondary exit from the house in the vicinity of the kitchen that can provide easy garbage and rubbish removal?

Another important aspect of the layout

is the traffic pattern. In an ideal world, you would not have to walk through any room to get to another. In practice, however, it doesn't usually work that way. One simple approach to minimize the effect of through traffic on a room is to locate the door toward a corner rather than in the center of the wall. That way traffic flows naturally around the sides of the room rather than through the heart of it.

A Little Talk About Scale I'm six feet seven inches, and people say that's tall. Well, yes, I suppose it is. But I still vividly remember a chance meeting with a seven-foot man in an elevator. I was stunned to speechlessness. Ever since, I've been a bit humble about my height. I'm not that tall, you know—tall is a relative concept.

Scale is about relative heights and widths and sizes. Scale—specifically, human scale—is an ever-present issue in thinking about house design and furniture. As with most of the considerations discussed in the last few pages, the final determinations are probably best left to an expert designer, but understanding scale may help you appreciate some of your needs—or what your architect does for you.

Scale and proportion work together. A cathedral ceiling is a visual essay in scale: look at me, it says, admire my sheer size. A cathedral ceiling in a tiny house says look at me—but does it also ask, "Why am I here?"

As you consider your house, think about how the different parts of it relate to one another. Are some very much out of proportion to others?

It is also important that you clearly understand what is being done for you. That is, when you get a sketch from your architect and you simply aren't sure what that 8-by-12-foot bedroom he has drawn is really like, measure one of your own and try to imagine what it would be like enlarged or shrunken to 8 by 12 feet. Scale is at issue in translating the precise drawings to the reality of the living space they represent.

Ceiling heights should be seen and not

merely imagined. Many building codes forbid ceilings lower than 7½ feet, so think of that as the minimum. But if you are considering a towering 20-foot ceiling, find one and experience it. You may discover that 12 feet is just as dramatic, or that the floor space in the room you are planning is dwarfed and you feel like you're in an upended shoe box rather than a palace.

What Are the Constraints?

We've talked about possibilities; you must also consider the limitations.

ZONING. If you are about to buy or have just bought your land, check with your broker regarding zoning requirements. Your lawyer, too, can do this research for you, but he'll charge you for his time and the real estate broker probably won't.

Some communities still have no zoning laws, but there are fewer of them every day. So anticipate that zoning requirements are a hurdle to be overcome.

Zoning ordinances usually specify four types of areas: residential, commercial, industrial, and agricultural. Each comes with restrictions, though the number of limitations decreases as you move from residential to the agricultural. Usually it is acceptable to build a house in any zone (should you want to), but while you can build "down" the zoning hierarchy, it is not generally acceptable to build "up."

Find out what the restrictions are. They can be an asset (who wants a landfill in the field behind the house?) or a hindrance ("What do you mean my wife can't sell antiques out of the garage?"). Make sure you know that the apartment you plan to put in that empty space over the garage can be rented out. If you live in a residential area zoned for single-family dwellings, it probably can't.

In addition to limiting industry, dumps, stores, and trailer parks, zoning regulations may specify minimum lot size and even house size. Zoning or municipal regulations are also likely to require certain setbacks (requirements that houses be a minimum distance from the street and property lines) and easements (rights of access that utilities and adjacent property owners have to some portion of the property that may limit the usefulness of that space).

Some zoning regulations specify maximum allowable lot coverage: whether you're adding on to your present home or building a new one, you may find that you will have to build up more than out to stay within the regulations. Maximum allowable heights are also common zoning regulations, as are parking requirements.

In some communities, you may find that in certain districts design standards are specified. A design review board may have to pass on your design; and they may not accept it. Find out first what the standards are and try to work within them.

If you find that you cannot work within the zoning requirement, you will need to apply for a zoning variance. Consult a local attorney who knows the ins and outs of the town or city's government and discuss the matter before proceeding with your plans or land purchase. In some areas variances are routine while in others they are as rare as .400 hitters.

While your broker or lawyer is asking these questions, find out about municipal water and sewage systems (if any). Inquire into gas, electric, and phone services as well.

RESTRICTIVE COVENANTS. If your project involves an addition to an existing house in a suburban development, you may have to consult with a jury of your neighbors.

Nearly three-quarters of all homes in recent suburban developments come complete with restrictions on what alterations can be made to the homes within the development's borders. While adherence to these restrictions is occasionally voluntary, more often the deed to each house will contain the binding rules or reference to them. In that case, the covenants are for all practical purposes laws you will have to abide by.

The regulations may be few or innu-

THE REAL ESTATE BROKER

If you are looking for a place to build or rebuild, you may want to consider getting a real estate broker to help you.

A broker costs you, the buyer, nothing since the seller pays the broker's fee. Yet a broker can do a great deal of the necessary legwork. He not only can find the right property but can gather information you need about zoning, municipal services, neighborhood values, and so on.

Find a broker you are comfortable with. Many are more interested in finding new sellers than in satisfying picayune buyers, so try to develop a relationship with a broker who understands your desires. At first, go with him to see that everything he suggests is right for you. Then give your broker a candid evaluation of what you've seen: if he's going to find the right spot for you, he has to get to know your tastes, including what you don't like as well as what you do.

Be realistic: if you never want to see a broker again, tell him that you're only willing to pay half the market value of a piece of property.

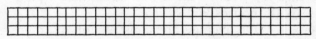

merable; frequently, the rules range widely over concerns as varied as the color of the house (usually a handful of colors are specified), the addition of such exterior amenities as pools, satellite dishes, basketball backboards, even mailboxes and house numbers. Additions large and small are almost always within the purview of such covenants.

In most cases, an architectural review board composed of laypersons and experts considers applications for changes. In order to add that garage, you will have to present your plans, detailing colors, materials, and other aspects.

If you have to go before such a board,

be sure your plans and specifications are clear, complete, and easy to read. Make it a point to know whether what you are requesting is specifically referred to in the covenants: know the rules before you go before the board. You should also be aware of what has already been done in your area. Precedents for your indoor, heated swimming pool will probably be helpful to you in making your case. And if all of the houses in your area are of a certain style and time, you might think twice before presenting plans for an addition that will seem out of sync with the rest.

HOW LONG WILL IT TAKE? No two projects are the same, so answers to questions of timing are necessarily vague. Nevertheless, a few generalizations may be helpful in thinking about the job you are facing.

Remodeling an existing space in your home is likely to take 2 to 6 months. This assumes no excavation is necessary.

Putting on an addition to your home may require 3 to 12 months.

Renovation of an old building will probably take longer, more like 6 to 18 months. This is perhaps the least predictable of the jobs. We all know people who have taken ten years to rehabilitate lovingly an old home; generally, using professional labor and a reasonable plan, 6 to 18 months will suffice.

On average, the construction of an entirely new home takes 1 to 2 years from conception to completion.

WHAT WILL IT COST? No book, no matter how complete, can give you much more than a wild approximation of what your job will cost. But a few guidelines may be helpful.

In most of the building trades the basis for estimating is cost per square foot. When you assemble a full range of estimates later (we will discuss that process in Chapter 4), you will have exact costs for each part of the construction. Average residential construction costs are almost impossible to estimate, given regional differences and other incalculable factors. In some parts of the South, you will pay $50 for what costs $150

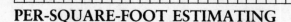

PER-SQUARE-FOOT ESTIMATING

RULE OF THUMB: The bigger the building, the lower the square-foot cost.

LABOR COSTS: Where the labor costs are higher, the square-foot cost will be higher, too. (Outside of major metropolitan areas, for example, labor savings equaling as much as 5 percent of the total cost of the home are not uncommon.)

REGIONAL DIFFERENCES: It is less expensive to build a house in the Deep South (Alabama and Mississippi, for example) than it is in California or the Northeast corridor (Boston, New York, or Philadelphia). What costs $1.00 in Montana will cost only about $0.75 in Tuscaloosa, but almost $1.25 in Boston and more like $1.50 in San Francisco. And the prices in Hawaii and Alaska are higher still.

QUALITY OF CONSTRUCTION: The materials you use and the laborers you hire are the two greatest determinants in the final price of your house. In fact, the square-foot cost for the same basic house can vary by 200 percent if expensive materials and labor-intensive designs are involved.

TOTAL NUMBER OF SQUARE FEET

Quality of Construction	750	1,000	1,250	1,500	1,750	2,000 and over
Class I	$79	$72	$69	$67	$65	$64
Class II	$58	$54	$52	$49	$47	$46
Class III	$41	$38	$36	$35	$34	$33

These per-square-foot estimates are based on 1986 prices.

In the table above, three classes of construction are specified. The Class I house is constructed of first-grade exterior materials (clapboards or brick) and has hardwood and tile floors, plaster

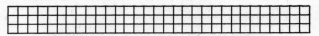

or skim-coated gypsum walls, and first-grade materials throughout. Class II is more likely to have a shingle or hardboard exterior, taped gypsum board on the walls, softwood or carpeted floors, and lower-cost kitchen and bathroom fixtures. A Class III house has lots of linoleum on the floors, composition siding, and appliances of minimum quality and number.

FOR REMODELING

According to a recent National Remodelers Council survey, the following are average remodeling prices for certain renovations:

ADDITIONS
One room	$30,103
Garage or porch	9,433
Bathroom	7,739
Fireplace	3,770

REMODELING OF
EXTANT SPACE
Bathroom	$ 7,739
Kitchen	12,430

FINISHING OF
PREVIOUSLY
UNFINISHED SPACE
Attic	$10,250
Basement	11,027

in the New York City area. In short, the variations are immense.

However, the likely range for typical residential construction is $40 to $75 per square foot. At the low end, you've got wall-to-wall carpeting and linoleum rather than hardwood and tile floors (and similar compromises in other materials and finishes).

Beginning the Paperwork

If you are remodeling an existing house rather than starting from scratch, it's a good idea to put on paper what you have and then begin the work of deciding what it is you want. In Chapter 2 we'll talk about the professionally executed plans you'll need for a building permit, but as a first step try to get a copy of the original plans for your house. The builder or architect may still be in business if it was constructed recently, and for a small charge they may be willing to provide you with photocopies of the blueprints. The building department may also have a set on file.

If, however, you cannot get a set of plans, it is not too great a task to make your own. You can address the problem yourself with graph paper. Available at any office or art supply store, standard graph paper with a ¼-inch grid is quite serviceable for drawing simple floor plans.

Do it to scale. If you are drawing a small house, use one square to a foot (that way a house or apartment that is roughly 25′ × 40′ fits on an 8 ½″ × 11″ sheet); if your house is larger, use a scale of 2 feet of house to each graph-paper square.

Don't concern yourself with wall thicknesses on your sketches unless the space is very tight and the loss or gain of half a foot is critical to the utility of a space. And don't bother with a ruler or T square; the graph-paper lines will keep your plan reasonably neat and square.

This process is especially useful when you are converting unfinished space or putting on a small addition. You should draw the whole house or apartment, including those sections that will remain unchanged. That way you have a basis for comparison: you will be able to get a sense of how much you will be gaining ("Did you realize, Frank, that that new bedroom for Junior is about the same size as our dressing room?").

Using this approach to the planning can be useful in a number of ways. Later, when you consult a professional, you can hand your draw-ings to your architect or designer if you wish. (Don't be insulted if he wants to double-check them himself.) It will save him some time, es-pecially if you are talking about renovation. In fact, if you have to pay him to do it, he might charge you as much as $500 for the time it takes him to measure and get basic dimensions like those you can collect yourself.

Another reason to do a quick floor plan for yourself is that no matter how long you've lived in the house or how sure you are of the dimensions of this or that space, you will cer-tainly discover things about the house that you didn't know before.

If you are planning to hire an architect to design an entirely new home for you, you may want to skip this step altogether. It's up to you. You may well learn something of your wants and wishes from trying it yourself (and your attempts may be helpful to the architect), but starting from scratch can be a daunting prospect indeed.

The Last Word Be sure to maintain a secure area for your plans, contracts, estimates, notes, correspondence, and the rest of your pa-perwork.

Keep it organized. Buy yourself a dozen or so plain manila folders and open up new files for each subject.

Don't throw anything away until at least a year after the job is completed and paid for. Even then, you may want to save much of the paperwork for tax reasons. Capital expend-itures can increase your property taxes, yet later can reduce the income taxes you pay on any cap-ital gains. Make sure you have all the paperwork to back you and your accountant up later on. It is certainly in your interest to save contracts, bills, guarantees, and other important documents in perpetuity.

When construction begins, you may want to have a traveling desk for your paper-work. A separate briefcase is a good idea, even if you routinely carry one for your work.

MEASURING A HOUSE

Your architect will do all this measuring for you, but he will probably charge you a half–day's labor for measuring an average-sized house. So save yourself a few hundred dollars—and get a better understanding of your house and your desires at the same time.

1. MATERIALS: You'll need two tape measures, one 50 feet long and another 12 feet; an 8 ½″ × 11″ pad of graph paper (¼″ or ⅛″ grid); and some pencils. A clipboard is also helpful.

2. THE OUTSIDE: Measure the perimeter of the house at the foundation level. Transfer these measurements to the graph paper, developing a two-dimensional scale drawing of the shape of the house as you go. Having a helper will save much time, not only for occasionally holding the other end of the tape but so that one person can write as the other calls out the measurements. Get your measurements accurate to ½″; don't worry about the quarters and eighths. Double-check everything.

Starting at each corner, measure the horizontal distance to each of the doors and windows (the distance is to the actual door or window sash, not the frames). Mark these, too, on your drawing.

Measure the building height, using your 12-foot tape. If the building is taller than your rule is long, determine how many clapboards or shingles or courses of brick there are for a given distance. If there are, say, 6 clapboards per 3 feet, and you count 36 between the ground and the roof, then you know the building is roughly 18 feet high.

Establish the location of the floor with respect to the point at which the siding and foundation join. Measure and record the distance from the bottom of the first clapboard or course of shingling or brick to the doorstep.

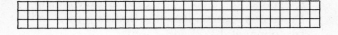

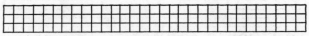

3. THE INSIDE: Measure the inside dimensions of all the rooms, from finished surface to finished surface (that is, wall to wall, not molding to molding). Measure the window heights from the floor; this, along with the floor-location measurement you made coming in, will later allow your architect to draw an elevation of the exterior.

Make sure you note all your wall thicknesses, too. It's easy to do at doorways.

Mark off all the fixed elements, including the furnace, plumbing fixtures, and appliances. Note especially plumbing pipes or vents that go up into any interior walls you are considering removing.

If you come across any signs of trouble— rot, uneven settlement (indicated by cracks in the foundation), cracked masonry (the mortar is falling out in chunks), leakage, or others—mark those, too, in your notes. When it is time to consult the experts about design and construction, get their opinions on the trouble spots. If you fix them now, the roof is less likely to fall in on your dreams later.

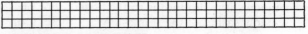

FLOOR-PLAN KITS

If you are not confident of your drafting abilities and are willing to spend about $25 to avoid the drawing, you can purchase a kit to do the job for you. Most come with a ruled layout sheet onto which you can place the treated vinyl symbols: first the walls go down, then you can position furniture and fixtures and your pool table in order to work out the best floor plan for your needs.

Check at your local architectural or art supply stores, as they may carry this variety of adult board game. If they don't, Hammacher Schlemmer in New York will sell you one by telephone (the model they carry is called "The Designer's Flexible Planning System"; their toll-free phone is 1-800-543-3366).

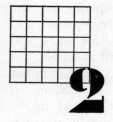

2 THE WORKING DRAWINGS

Communicating Your Dream to the Professionals

Defining the word "architecture" is rather like trying to define the word "home." A home is a dwelling, yet it is also a great deal more than simply a house. In the same way, architecture is usually a building—but by no means are all buildings truly architecture.

The word "architect" meant "master builder" in its original classical Greek. The architect you hire should indeed be a master builder in the sense that he or she must design you a building that meets your needs for shelter and temperature control and provides you with spaces for sleeping, eating, working, and playing. Yet the same "master builder" you hire works in a profession whose association in this country, the American Institute of Architects, for most of this century specifically prohibited its members from themselves building anything.

The architect's role has been transformed since the Greeks coined the title to describe him. The architect is no longer a master builder: he is much more likely to be a technocrat whose major concern is with complying with the immense variety of rules and regulations and with properly using the incredible wealth of building materials and equipment available. Yet we still expect the architect to be a practitioner of a fine art, and charge him or her with an obligation to create an edifice that through its design and ornamentation is aesthetically pleasing.

Actually, the architect is something of an enigma. He or she is, in some ways, an artist whose flights of creative fancy you want to utilize. In other ways, the architect is a sophisticated estimator and buyer of services (i.e., a businessman) who must be as concerned with suiting the limitations of your pocketbook as he is with pleasing your eye. And your architect must have the technical know-how to design a building that will stand up to your use and the elements' abuse.

Clearly, contradictions abound when you try to maneuver the architect into a definable niche. For our purposes, let us take a simple approach: an architect is one whose task it is to create environments. Some do it well, some don't; some do it to our tastes, some not. But at the most fundamental level, the architect is concerned with designing buildings that serve the needs of their denizens. That is a more practical, contemporary definition of an architect's role.

Robert W. Knight is an architect who trained at Yale, then worked and taught in California. Now he practices in Maine, and his specialty is residential architecture. "I figure most everybody has a house in his head," he says of the typical client, "but not everybody has the skills and the training to put it on paper or translate it to a builder; and that's what I am—the bridge. My ideal trip is to find the house that they can't even see, add my skills to make it cohesive and affordable, and get it onto paper. So when they come in they say, 'Wow! There it is, that's the house I've been dreaming about, but I couldn't quite tell you.' "

Chapter 1 was about establishing your needs and desires. The purpose of this chapter is to help you find the "bridge" you need to exchange your ideas and rough sketches for detailed working drawings that can be the basis for accurately estimating and, eventually, constructing your home space.

Do I Really Need Professional Help?

Well, quite frankly, no law says you have to have an architect or designer.

On the other hand, you will need plans. Most building codes require detailed plans and close adherence to regulations regarding wiring, plumbing, structure, and so on. Your bank, moreover, is unlikely to lend you money unless you have specific, professionally prepared plans. Further, detailed specifications listing materials are necessary for getting accurate cost estimates. Whether they are the product of your hand or someone else's, you need plans.

If you have design skills, you may wish to take on the task yourself. But how sure are you that you know enough to do the job? The simplest definition of the requisite "design skills" is that you have had the training to execute professional-quality architectural drawings. If you cannot honestly claim this qualification, you probably shouldn't try to do it on your own. If your design skills are such that you can draw the plans but you do not have a real knowledge of house construction and of the building trades, getting a pro is still a good idea, particularly since the regulations in many communities require that all plans bear the stamp of a licensed architect or engineer.

On the other hand, if you are building a house from scratch, you have the option of buying a stock plan. We'll talk about those in some detail shortly, as they can be a very practical alternative to hiring an architect or designer (see page 58). If you use a stock plan as is, no architect will be necessary.

However, if you want a custom-designed house; if you are planning a substantial restoration or remodeling of your present home;

in short, if you need a plan to follow and there isn't a ready-made one available, you need help.

Why not just hire a contractor and let him do the design? You can: People do it all the time. An experienced contractor, in fact, may be as well equipped to deal with a straightforward design as an architect. But if there are any out-of-the-ordinary wrinkles or peculiarities in your design, you may discover to your disadvantage your contractor's limitations as a designer.

Few builders are designers; almost none would pretend to you that they are. Architects and designers specialize in the abstract, in conceiving suitable configurations, shapes, and spaces. Builders are concerned with the concrete details of materials and fasteners and with the physical work of construction. While most general contractors have a stock plan or two in their files from which they have worked in the past, few are trained to create a design themselves.

The architect is a forest-through-the-trees person. It is the carpenter's and other tradesmen's jobs to be concerned with the individual constituent parts; it is the architect's responsibility to envision the whole.

Expert advice is just as important in remodeling as in new construction, for both design and structural reasons. For example, if you are considering the removal of a wall, you will have to establish that it is not a "bearing wall" that is crucial to carrying the weight of the structure above to the foundation below. Issues having to do with foundations and heating capacities and innumerable others have to be considered.

Design issues, too, have to be resolved: they are as important to the resale value of your house as structural matters. You will cost yourself money in the long term if you remodel your house (or "remuddle" it, as the parlance of the renovation business now terms it) by violating the integrity of the house's original design, if you turn the place into a neighborhood eyesore, or even if you simply make the sort of small mistakes that are to be expected of the untrained designer. Examples of such mistakes are doors that open into other doors; mixed-up window shapes that seem fine from inside but look all out of proportion from without; ideas adapted from magazines that looked just right in their original settings but seem grossly out of place in your house.

If you are still unsure whether you want an architect or not, consider the following story.

Kevin Jordan went to a local contractor near his home just outside Denver, Colorado. He asked the contractor—the father of a college friend and a man he knew and trusted—to build him a home.

The contractor (let's call him Josh) pulled out the several plans he had used in recent projects. Kevin chose the one he liked, and Josh worked up an estimate for him. He found a bank willing to give him a mortgage.

Kevin already owned the piece of property, so things moved quickly. Ground-breaking day was almost upon them when Kevin's wife announced that she was expecting their second child. The news was a surprise, but just in time. It's easier to put another bedroom into a house that isn't built yet than into one that's finished.

Josh and Kevin pored over the plans. Josh suggested that the best solution was a bigger house, and gave Kevin an estimate for what it would cost. Kevin, already nervous at the anticipated expense of the new baby, was reluctant to assume an even greater financial burden.

At the suggestion of a friend, he consulted a local architect. The architect looked at the plans and discussed with Kevin and his wife their problems and concerns. The architect suggested a couple of small changes—the outside dimensions of the house remained the same but the configuration of the rooms within was changed. He also brought to Kevin's attention a few details in materials that Kevin hadn't noticed and suggested some substitutes.

The architect charged Kevin at an hourly rate; he solved the problem to Kevin's satisfaction; he improved the finish with his detail suggestions. The cost? Essentially nothing: the architect's fee was several thousand dollars less than the estimated cost of the extra space the builder suggested adding.

This is not always the case. In fact, the chances are that hiring an architect will add to your total cost. And there are prima donna architects who are more concerned with their own aesthetics than they are with their clients' pocketbooks. But it is also true that architects have training that enables them to see spaces in a way that the untrained eye cannot. Some of this is the result of learning the rules, some of it instinct, some of it experience.

Let's look at another example or two. One set of design rules involves what is known as the "kitchen triangle." This refers to the location of the three principal areas of activity in the kitchen: the sink, stove, and refrigerator. There are many possible configurations for any kitchen, but the best way to approach the problem is to arrange the key areas into a triangle whose perimeter is not more than 22 feet, with the individual work areas being roughly 5 to 9 feet apart. The kitchen triangle is an eminently workable solution to a multitude of different design problems, and it is a rule that architects—and thoughtful contractors—know and follow.

A good architect/designer also has a body of experience to draw upon. When you look at the rabbit warren of tiny upstairs bedrooms in the old house you just bought, you may understand intellectually that there are many possibilities there. But the professional may see immediately that the addition of a dormer here, the removal of a wall there, the construction of a new knee wall at that point, and presto, in his mind's eye, a brightly lit studio appears. To you, there are possibilities you can't quite see; to the architect, it's a matter of developing a clear image that can be put on paper. Then you get to review the possibilities come to life.

By that point, the designer will have worked through a number of potential hassles you might not have considered until it was too late. For example, is there an alternate exit in your plan—a second staircase or at least a large window or fire escape—in the event of a fire on the second floor? Each bedroom should have an accessible fire escape route. Your architect will be aware of these and innumerable other considerations.

The bottom line? If your project is very straightforward and requires essentially no imaginative brainstorming, you may be quite satisfied with the standard structure your contractor offers to build for you. But if you want something out of the ordinary, you need a professional to guide you in the design of your new house or addition. And sometimes he pays for himself simply by helping you avoid costly mistakes and ensuring that you get what you want . . . not what you think you want.

On the other hand, if you are hiring an architect to administrate construction so you can be confident the job is being done right, keep in mind that most architect's contracts call for virtually all of the architect's fee to be paid before construction begins. This doesn't necessarily mean your architect will pay little more than lip service to on-site inspections; in fact, many architects and contractors acknowledge that the give-and-take of a designer/builder collaboration produces better buildings. However, you may want to consider hiring an architect or other professional as a "construction manager." This way you are not paying for design time you don't want but you will get the attentive inspections you need. We'll talk more of this arrangement in later chapters.

So weigh your needs. If you have a stock plan that you do not intend to amend, you don't need design help. If your contractor has just the right house for you, hire him to build it. But if you want something you can't quite see or something requiring some development or design finesse, talk to an architect.

How Much Will It Cost?

The title "architect" conjures up in many people's minds fancy designer houses. People think of Frank Lloyd Wright and expensive, one-of-a-kind homes on private hilltops for movie stars and the super-rich.

It's true, people with a great deal of money often hire architects. But it isn't true that you have to be rich to afford one. In fact, architects can save the client money, as in Kevin's case.

They know the business of building. They know how much things cost and can make the most of what their clients can afford. An architect, like any professional, relies upon referrals for new clients, and the client whose house was substantially over budget isn't going to recommend its designer to his worst enemy.

You pay an architect to perform several different tasks. We will discuss these tasks at length later in this chapter, but in general you will be paying him to devise a general approach for you; to create some preliminary drawings; and to execute finished drawings. The last part is roughly half the job, the first two something like 25 percent each.

That presupposes you don't hire your architect to see the job all the way through. If he does, he will want roughly another 20 percent.

Architect's fees vary from job to job. Most will offer you a choice of a fixed design fee, a percentage of construction, or an hourly basis for billing.

Fixed Fee. The fixed fee is just what the name suggests, an arrangement in which the architect and the client agree to a single price for the job. They also agree on what the job is, so if there is a significant change from the original agreement (say, the house doubles in size or budget), then the fee may be renegotiated. Otherwise, the fee agreed upon on day one should be the fee the client pays.

Percentage of Budgeted Construction Cost. This is perhaps the most common method of paying an architect. The fee will be a percentage of the total construction cost, generally 10 to 15 percent in residential construction. The greater the cost of construction, the lower the percentage the fee should be.

The key word here is "budgeted." That means that if you determine before breaking ground that the total cost is to be, say, $100,000, then it is the architect's job to design a house that costs $100,000, and his percentage will be based on that sum. However, if the job ends up costing $125,000, there is no reason why he should be rewarded by being paid the same percentage of the higher cost, especially if he has been in charge of the process from the start. (One exception would be, however, where the cost overrun was the result of the client's making changes and adjustments along the way. In such cases, it is reasonable for the architect to expect additional payment for his additional services.)

Whatever the method of payment, the architect will want, as mentioned above, the bulk of his fee upon completion of the plans. If you do not plan to involve him in the administration of the construction, he'll want it all. After all, whether he is to be at your side throughout the process or not, he will have done most of his job by the time the finished drawings are complete.

Sometimes special deals can be made. One instance I know of was a model house in a newly developed beachfront on the Virginia shore. The first house to be built was architect-designed, and the architect agreed to a greatly reduced fee (only about 5 percent of construction cost). It made sense to him because he was new to the area; because the house was located at the very entrance to the site where a number of other beautiful lots were for sale; and because he felt he had the perfect design for the spot, a project he had begun in architecture school years before.

It worked out. The architect to date has gotten two commissions for other houses in the development (at full rate), and the customer in the first house is thrilled with his original and comfortable home.

HOURLY WAGE. Some architects will work on an hourly basis. This method of payment is common in renovation or remodeling jobs.

If you opt for this arrangement, consider writing two safeguards into your understanding. First, negotiate an "upset price" into the agreement. We will discuss upset prices for construction contracts in detail in Chapter 5, but the concept is simple and sensible. You and the architect agree on a maximum fee; further, you agree on an hourly rate. Then he keeps track of the hours required to complete the job. If his hourly wages are less than the upset price, you pay the lower sum, but if they are more, that's his problem. You do not pay any more than the ceiling (the upset price) you agreed upon at the start.

The other safeguard (not only for this agreement but for any agreement, as we'll discuss in Chapter 5) is a clearly stated payment schedule. You should agree to pay the architect for performance. Perhaps a small payment is due on signing of the contract, another on acceptance of the preliminary sketches, and so on. In this way, the architect gets paid as he works, but you also know exactly what you are paying for.

OTHER EXPENSES. It is common for architects to bill you separately for extra expenses. These include reproduction costs (photocopying of blueprints), which shouldn't be more than $500; engineering costs when the services of a specially trained structural engineer are required (an unusual design configuration and an addition to an older home which requires the existing structure to bear some of its weight are two circumstances that might call for such a consultation; the prices vary greatly, so be sure your architect gives you an estimate up front); the costs of a survey to determine the boundaries or contours or other aspect of your property (this may be required if you are building a new home or putting on an addition). As with engineering fees, get an estimate from your architect first.

Which Professional Is Best?

THE ARCHITECT. The architectural profession requires of its members an unusual blend of the creative and the pragmatic. A good architect must have both an artist's eye for shapes and color and an accountant's expertise for balancing budgets. Like a chess player who must be able to anticipate many moves ahead, the architect must be able to envision the space he or she is shaping and anticipate the traffic patterns and airflow and the interrelationship of innumerable other factors. As if that is not enough, the architect must also conceive a design that suits your subjective tastes.

An architect must be licensed in your state. To qualify for the licensing examination, he must have at least a bachelor's degree in architecture and three years' experience working in an architect's office. A registered architect must take legal responsibility for his work.

The architect's training involves a varied and complex curriculum. Courses in the strength of materials are just as important as those in design, as the most elegant structure in the land isn't worth anything if it won't survive the next heavy snowfall or gale-force wind. The architect must know not only how materials look but how they are to be used. He will be able to advise you on what materials distinctions really mean (e.g., using cedar shakes instead of asphalt shingles on your roof will cost you more initially, but the life expectancy of the more expensive material is substantially greater, too).

THE DESIGNER/DRAFTSMAN. There are no licensing requirements for designers in most states. Theoretically, you and I could hang a shingle out tomorrow and call ourselves designers. Thus it is doubly important that you thoroughly establish the experience and proven abilities of any designer before hiring.

As a rule, home designers are less expensive than fully trained and licensed architects. Their work may or may not be as good. But a key consideration has to be how complex the job you are considering is. If it involves some unusual structural elements or a setting that demands special strategies, be sure your designer/draftsman has all the requisite expertise in solving these special problems. Architects and designers alike consult structural engineers when the going gets complicated. Ask your designer if he has consulted such an expert if your design involves out-of-the-ordinary or outsized shapes.

STOCK PLANS AND KIT HOUSES. If you are building a new house, you have an alternative to hiring a pro to design it for you. There are thousands of stock plans available, with complete plans usually costing in the range of $100 to $150. Sets of five or more copies are available at a discount (you'll need more than one to service the needs of the carpenter, electrician, building department, and others).

One example of how and why stock plans are used is shown by Sarah and Joseph Smithson. Joe's business having skyrocketed in the late seventies, they were in a position to buy their dream house.

Sarah is from New England and always wanted to live in a saltbox home. The problem was that Sarah and Joe lived in Ohio and there simply weren't any to be had. They both thought of themselves as do-it-yourselfers (Joe had started his business on $5,000 borrowed from an uncle), so when they decided to build, they felt that hiring an architect would have been "cheating."

They ordered catalogues from several mail-order house-plan companies. They didn't find exactly the house they wanted, but they found one that was the right size and had the right exterior shape and proportions. They bought the plans for $110 and hired a house designer to move a couple of rooms around (Joe wanted a large office, Sarah demanded a half bath off the kitchen). The designer charged them $1,500 plus copying expenses. For $1,723.40, they had their design.

Stock plans are, in short, an inexpensive alternative to hiring an architect. Yet they also offer the option of deciding for yourself what you want. Whereas the house that the contractor builds for you is most likely to have come from a file of house plans in his desk drawer, with stock plans you can select almost any conceivable style.

Stock plans can be a workable alternative even if no stock plan provides exactly what you want. In a situation where a standard plan comes close, you can do what Sarah and Joe did and hire an architect or designer/draftsman to amend the plan. In that case, the cost will be limited to the hours spent changing the plan and will be much lower than if you have an architect create a design for you from scratch.

With stock plans, however, it's more difficult to incorporate more than a few of your own design ideas. And you won't get a unique house, as stock plans tend to be of sound but rather traditional layout and design. If your house is going to cost you $200,000 or $300,000, then perhaps the saving of a few thousand dollars is less important than that the house possess the special originality and personality you desire.

If you do opt for a stock plan, be sure to check with your local building department to see that all aspects of the plan meet local building code requirements.

Another alternative to hiring an architect is the prefabricated house. These come in a variety of designs, but, to my way of thinking, the old saw "you get what you pay for" holds true here. The prefab house does cost less, but its design and configuration are limited by the mode of delivery. After all, prefabs are delivered preassembled on the bed of a truck. In my experience, they don't offer the same permanence or flexibility that a traditionally constructed house does.

On the other hand, a more satisfactory alternative is a so-called kit house. Also known as manufactured houses, kit houses are, as their name suggests, made up of ready-to-assemble components that are precut and marked at the factory and shipped to you, complete with instructions. For obvious reasons, they are a sen-

SOURCES FOR MAIL-ORDER PLANS

Most magazines concerned with home design and decoration will have advertisements for makers of mail-order plans. In particular, be on the lookout for annual special issues of *House Beautiful, Home Magazine,* and *Better Homes and Gardens* that may feature a number of the stock-plan designs. A few of the well-known stock-plan publishers are:

Home Planners, Inc., 23761 Research Drive, Farmington Hills, Michigan 48024. Their publications include *120 Early American Home Plans* and *144 Home Designs for All Americans.*

Larry Garnett Associates, 3515 Preston Road, Pasadena, Texas 27505. They publish portfolios in a variety of styles, from what they term "Victorian" to "Garden," "Traditional," and "French."

L. F. Garlinghouse Company, 34 Industrial Park Place, Middletown, Connecticut 06457. Garlinghouse has been selling a variety of plans since 1920.

National Plan Service, 435 West Fullerton Avenue, Elmhurst, Illinois 60126-1498.

If you are unable to find any of these companies' publications in your local bookstore or library or ads for them in a home magazine, you can request a catalogue by mail. There may be a charge of a few dollars for the catalogue, but it will provide floor plans and simple elevations of each design that should be sufficient for you to make a choice. Once you decide on the one you want, you can order the complete plans.

sible choice for homeowners with construction skills.

Kit homes were popular back at the turn of the century when Sears, Roebuck & Company sold its brand of Honor-Bilt Modern Homes. The

Sears catalogue offered twenty-two different models, with prices ranging from $2,500 for a Queen Anne-style house to as little as $650 for a three-room bungalow. Over the next thirty-plus years, Sears sold more than 100,000 construction kit homes and, though Sears abandoned the business in 1940, since World War II a variety of other manufacturers have appeared that sell a great variety of dwellings.

The virtue of the best kit homes is that they can be assembled quickly and at lower cost than can an architect/contractor home constructed from scratch. They are not uniformly well made, however, and not all arrive with every piece cut and ready to attach. But some kit-home manufacturers offer a variety of high-quality options, from hand-hewn beams to mahogany doors.

The process of buying a kit home bears some resemblance to the process of buying a stock plan for your house. With a kit home, the manufacturer offers certain standard models. You may modify them to suit your tastes, but most manufacturers charge an additional fee for converting your sketches into blueprints and tailoring the materials to your specs. It may make sense to hire an architect to design your desired layout changes within the standard plans, but be sure you get a written estimate from the manufacturer of what the changes will cost before you sign the contract.

Perhaps most important of all, you should arrange to see a finished house from the kit maker of your choice. That's the only way to get a clear idea of what the final product will be like. You should take that opportunity to question the homeowner (especially if he was the assembler) about how the pieces fit together, what problems were encountered, whether delivery was on time, and so on.

Kit houses can include everything down to the switch cover for the dimmer switch in the dining room or can be limited to a bare shell. While log homes are the most common kind of kit home sold in this country, you can also buy

A-frames and post-and-beam structures and numerous other varieties. For a list of some 150 makers of manufactured housing, send $1.00 and a stamped, self-addressed envelope to the Building Institute, Piermont, New York 10968.

Once you have decided upon the kit house you want, the process is much the same as for a traditional house: you'll need to obey building codes, hire contractors, get financing, supervise construction, and follow the advice given in the next chapter.

Finding the Right Architect

In an ideal world, you would ask a trusted friend or relative who it was he used to design that new house you so much admire. That friend or relative would give you the architect's name and an enthusiastic endorsement of his skills and reasonableness. Then you'd call that architect and get on with it.

We don't live in an ideal world, but your best source is still a personal reference. If a friend, relative, or neighbor has recently had his home built or remodeled, ask for his assessment of the designer he used. Chances are you will get an unprejudiced evaluation—he likes the result or he doesn't, the architect/designer was helpful and responsive or he wasn't, and so on. Occasionally you will get an insecure response from someone who isn't really satisfied with what he bought but is unwilling to acknowledge it because to do so would be to admit having made a mistake. But generally you'll get a pretty candid earful, and you can also get a look at the architect's work to help you make up your mind.

If you can't think of an acquaintance who has used an architect, then ask the professionals whose business it is to deal with architects. Your banker or your real estate broker may be able to recommend someone. The yellow pages will surely offer up a few candidates, as will the Better Business Bureau in your area and the National Association of the Remodeling Industry, and you can always check with the

American Institute of Architects (1735 New York Avenue, Washington, D.C. 20006) for the licensed architects in your area. They can refer you to the local chapter and perhaps to a subcommittee on single-family residential design. A contractor friend may have a suggestion or two, but beware of any disparaging comments he may make. Architects and contractors are like playwrights and directors. The playwright knows what he meant, the director how to get it across to the audience; they need each other, but many directors are a lot happier directing plays by long-dead playwrights. Their work is proven, and they don't complain anywhere near as much.

Once you have a candidate or two, don't think for a minute you are home free. Now your homework really begins, as not every architect is good, and fewer still are likely to be suited to your tastes and personality.

Make an appointment to see the architect. Visit his office. Talk about your needs and concerns and get a sense of him personally and professionally. Talk about fees, too, as it is never too early to broach this subject. You don't have to resolve it down to the last dollar and cent on day one, but don't allow the subject to be shunted aside with assurances like "That's no problem, I'm sure we can work that out."

You will have to make a judgment about whether the architect is right for you or not. Among the other factors that can be helpful in making that decision are these:

Previous Work. Ask to see what he has done before. Does it suggest the quality and style of home you are considering? He may have a portfolio to show you with photographs and drawings, or even models you can admire. Start with those, but, if at all possible, see the work in person.

Get the names and addresses of some of his clients. Make appointments to look at the work and talk to the clients themselves. Ask the homeowners how smoothly the job went, whether it came in on budget, how flexible the architect was in dealing with the client's and the contractor's questions and problems. The architect is unlikely to send you to see work that either he or the customer is dissatisfied with, but you can still learn a lot from looking and talking.

Checking references is the best single safeguard you have. At the same time, however, experience is not the only indicator of ability. A young, energetic architect may be willing to do more research and may bring fresher ideas than the old pro with an established, staid practice. But here again, you must rely on your good judgment. Experience is very valuable but not an absolute prerequisite.

Make sure the architect does a good deal of residential work. If there's only one house and twenty factories in his portfolio, that should tell you something. Residential work can be very satisfying for an architect, but it is likely to be more time-consuming than profitable. If he hasn't done many homes, ask why.

Staff. Try to determine whether the architect has adequate staff and a work load that will allow for the proper amount of personal attention to the project from start to finish. Ask him how many meetings he thinks will be necessary; how many design hours he anticipates.

Accessibility. Does the location of the architect's office make it possible for him to be available for consultations? If you plan to involve your architect in overseeing construction, will he have to travel an hour each way to get to the job site? A long trek back and forth may mean fewer inspections, or perhaps larger, portal-to-portal billings.

On the other hand, don't reject an architect whose work you like simply because of geography. I know of one case where an architect in Rensselaer, New York, designed and supervised the construction of a timber-frame studio in Minnesota. The architect, Janet Null, says of the distance from office to work site, "It's a little bit of a problem, but not insurmountable. It really depends on the scale of the project."

Working with an Architect

Once you have found an architect, you must determine whether you can work with him. If you are uncomfortable with him (or her) for any reason—say, if you are both highly strung creative individuals and you can foresee getting into long, hard-fought struggles about every detail—perhaps you should continue your search.

This is probably the most arbitrary decision in a series of subjective decisions, but it may be the most important. Your experience of overseeing the design and construction of some or all of your living space can be immensely satisfying and exciting. Particularly if you plan to ask your architect to stay with the project through to the end, make sure you are confident that he is willing to listen to what you say and to try to accommodate your concerns. You will have to trust his judgment, too, so be sure that you feel in your heart as well as in your head that he is well suited to the job at hand.

Your first meeting with him is, in large part, about personalities, as you must establish some sort of rapport with one another. You want to impart to him a sense of what you want, but your notes and sketches and future discussions will do that.

You should also emerge from your first meeting with a specific understanding as to the fee schedule. That doesn't mean necessarily that you will have a total price for all architectural services from the start through to the completion of the house, but at least you should know what will be the cost of developing a design and executing the working drawings. He should warn you about the cost of changes and where costs can escalate as the design process gets further advanced.

Given the exploratory nature of the first meeting, there should be no charge for that session.

You should know that if you decide to walk away after, say, the first schematic drawings have been presented to you, you will owe him a certain sum. Having discussed fees with him at your first meeting, there should be no financial surprises. The sooner you reach an understanding with him, the better.

If you feel comfortable with your architect, give him your notes after your first meeting. Give him your answers to the questionnaire in Chapter 1, your figurings on total square feet in the house, any floor plans you've drawn, and any pictures or other research you've done into your ideal house. If the job involves adding to an existing house, he will need its plans and photographs and other materials to orient him to the extant space. He will certainly want to look at it firsthand, too.

Talk to him about needs and limitations. If you begin by talking to several architects, you probably would do best to pick the one you like, and then let him go at your problem—you don't want to pay for each of them to work for you, do you? On the other hand, if you have a particular design problem, you needn't feel shy about turning two or three architects loose, so long as there is a cap on what each architect's initial presentation will cost. In the case of one kitchen renovation I've seen in a small city apartment, the strategy worked well. The owner told me two of the architects came up with workable solutions (the third was of no value, in his judgment). And the one he chose to proceed with worked out very well.

Reviewing the Plans

Bob and Linda had purchased their small Cape as a young, newly married couple. They had made it their own in the ten years they had lived there, remodeling the kitchen, removing a partition between the dining and living rooms, and making other changes. It was a practical, comfortable house for two professional people.

When their baby, Caitlin, arrived, things changed. They simply needed more space. Their previous changes hadn't altered the basic structure of the house, but this time an addition was required. They decided to hire an architect.

Before they did, they thought long and hard about what they liked about their house, what the strengths and weaknesses of it were, and what purposes they wanted the new space to serve.

They decided that the new space they needed was a family room. While for them the two existing bedrooms were quite adequate, the rooms were rather small and Bob and Linda felt that a potential buyer some years down the road might want something bigger. So they decided to have the family room designed in such a way that it could be a master bedroom suite for the next owners. They needed the extra bath anyway, they reasoned.

By the time they hired the architect, they had quite definite notions of what they wanted. They met with the architect in their home, and he looked around thoroughly. He measured the existing building, and he asked Bob and Linda many questions about their lifestyle (did they eat breakfast? in which room?) and about their tastes, habits, and budget. They told him in detail what they wanted. They even told him about some ideas they had rejected, one of which was to put the addition on a diagonal from the axis of the existing house.

The architect went away and came back with detailed drawings. Not content with a floor plan, he did elevations, too. The addition had a spiral staircase and a 20-foot cathedral ceiling in the new room. And the addition went off on a diagonal.

Bob and Linda were, at first, struck dumb. They were quite impressed. They enjoy entertaining and the new space would be a spectacular showplace for guests. But a bedroom with a 20-foot ceiling seemed a little odd, especially in cold New England with its high energy costs.

It was the angle of the building that finally decided it for them, however. They had specifically told him not to design it that way, having already learned from a contractor friend that the construction costs would be considerably greater given the difficulties in framing presented by the oddball angles. The design was original and very appealing, but it really didn't relate to their needs.

They sent the architect back to the drawing board. He lowered the roofline so that the new room had a traditional ceiling height. The building went off the existing house at a simple right angle. The architect had to invest a few hours of drafting time gratis since his redrawing time raised his total hours beyond his original estimate, but it didn't cost Bob and Linda anything, since they had negotiated an upset price into their agreement.

If they were doing it all over, would they use an architect again? Bob feels a sense of conflict about that issue. He would do it differently, perhaps, but the fact is that the more they live in the house, the more they realize the architect had thought about many details, which, at first, had not been apparent but which make the house more comfortable and easier to live in. But he is quick to add that the contractor also added a good many improvements that the architect had not thought of.

Different architects work in different ways.

Some will show very preliminary sketches that look more like doodles than architectural drawings. In Bob and Linda's case, everybody probably would have been better off if more preliminary sketches had made it to their coffee table earlier.

Early sketches are often abstract, rough pencil jottings meant to suggest an approach that is not so much visual as intellectual; it is a framework with which the architect will approach the project. If your architect begins with such rough drawings, you will not see any sense of style, dimension, or even shape but will be asked to think about the doodles as representing in a thematic way the nature of the space you are building, the traffic patterns through it, and the relationships of the spaces within to one another. The only realistic aspect is likely to be the determination of whether there are one or more stories.

Your architect, particularly if the paperwork you give him clearly spells out your desires, may arrive with drawings that are recognizable as floor plans.

When your architect has plans to show you, the usual practice is for you to sit down and review them with him. He will explain his intent in executing the design as he has, and discuss with you any reactions you have.

You've given him your notes, so what he gives back to you should be familiar. If at first you don't see in his drawings what you saw in yours, focus on what is different. Are they better in some ways but not in others? Ask your architect to explain to you what his rationale is for what he has done.

In part, the point here is to be open-minded. You must give your designer the opportunity to respond to your material. Pay him the courtesy of listening to him as he did to you. Your architect will have taken your materials and will have absorbed what you said. He will have applied his own training, experience, and instincts. Even if at first you don't like what he has done, give it a chance.

It is also very important to inquire about anything you don't understand.

PRELIMINARY SKETCHES. They should look familiar to you. Not that you've seen them before, but they are at least in part supposed to be a product of your ideas.

If the first sketches do not look like what you were seeing in your mind's eye, try to look through whatever details of finish that the architect has added. Do you see the same shapes and relationships you discussed earlier? If there has been a major departure, ask why.

Ask yourself if the design answers your needs. If not, say so.

It's a good idea for you to live with a set of the preliminary sketches for a day or two before giving your architect your formal response. Have others in your household study them, too. The architect will no doubt take notes on your reactions as he shows them to you and you express concerns about the size of this or the absence of that. However, almost invariably your response a day or two later is more reasoned, thoughtful, and complete than at the moment you are confronted with new shapes and thoughts and visions.

It creates headaches for everybody to have friends or relatives kibbitzing ("I wouldn't do it that way if I were you"). But if you are not confident of your feelings about how the plan is emerging, you may wish to involve one outsider whose tastes are compatible with your own. Take care not to let that person dominate you. It is, after all, going to be your house.

When you do discuss things with your designer, have written notes to guide you. An elaborately phrased, typed letter is unnecessary, but having a carefully assembled list is important. That way you won't forget something and you will have an idea of the volume of issues you are raising. You may even discover before you talk with the architect that there is a pattern to the problems, so that one general comment can be made that covers a number of smaller issues.

Be candid with your architect. Don't get personal if you really dislike something, but be frank and say it doesn't work for you. If it doesn't work at all, say so, but at the same time be sure your response is a fair one. Just because it isn't what you expected doesn't mean it's bad. It could be better than your original notion—after all, you have hired a professional to do the best job he can, and maybe with his training and experience he can see things you could not. Give it fair consideration.

Be as articulate as you can about why something is unsatisfying to you. The more specific you can be about your objections, the more likely it is that he will be able to make the changes you want in the next set of plans.

As you consider the plans, think about the lives and schedules and habits of the people who will be living there. Imagine yourself in each doorway, seated in every corner. What do you see in the room, out the windows, looking down the hallways?

If you like what you see, don't hesitate to say so. Architects appreciate approval just as much as other people.

PRELIMINARY PLANS. How many sets of plans will you see? The earliest drawings will be the most generalized and are as much for discussion as anything. It may take one or many sets of rough sketches before you are satisfied with the direction the building is going. But once you are confident with the overall shape and size, it's time to go on to preliminary plans.

If you see several sets of preliminary plans, each set should have more detail than the last and should incorporate the changes you discussed in the previous versions. However, before the preliminary plans give way to the final plans and specifications, you should get your architect's best estimates of the total cost. It is never too early to talk about budget (construction budget rather than design fee), as your architect should know from your first session what your financial range is. But at this point it is realistic to get specific about costs.

At this stage, the "working systems"— the electrical, plumbing, and heating and air-conditioning systems—enter the picture. (Heating and air conditioning is often termed HVAC.) Decisions about specific materials, too, are useful at this point. Doors, windows, wall coverings, and so on factor in here. This is also the stage (if you are constructing a new home or putting on a major addition) when your architect prepares "outline specs" (preliminary listings of materials and instructions used for purposes of estimating).

Some clients or architects will choose to ask a contractor to join in at this stage. (We will talk more about the contractor and his role in Chapter 4.) A contractor can be useful at this time for estimating purposes. In addition, he may be able to draw on his personal experience to offer solutions to certain problems that your architect might not come up with.

Before instructing the architect/designer to execute the final plans, you should study the last set of preliminary plans one room at a time. Make sure your furniture fits. Check the location of every light fixture and every plug; are there enough of them? Again, imagine yourself living in the space: does it all seem to be as you want it?

FINAL PLANS AND SPECIFICATIONS. These large pieces of paper are, finally, what you are paying your architect for. It is the final drawings and numbers and lists that will enable your contractor first to estimate accurately what it all will cost and then to construct what has been so laboriously planned. The following portfolio of plans will give you some idea of what to expect of the final plans.

Review the set of plans carefully (before you sign any construction contracts). Make sure it is consistent with the last version you saw, and that the corrections you asked for have been made. Make sure you understand absolutely everything. It will cost you extra money later if you want something changed that you, out of ignorance, let pass at an earlier stage. Even substantial changes are relatively inexpensive before the contracts are signed and the hammers begin to swing.

In the case of a job where new construction is being incorporated into an extant building, make sure that the old is accurately represented. Are the windows and doors in the right places?

Keep a rule handy as you review plans. It may even make sense to buy an inexpensive architect's scale (a plastic one can be purchased at most art supply stores for a few dollars). It is helpful when reviewing the plans. Use it to get a sense of the dimensions at hand.

Crucial to working with an architect—and, eventually, with any contractors you hire to do the actual construction—is mastering the art of compromise.

No matter how reasonable you are and how professional your designer is, you are going to have different feelings about things. If he's any good, he's going to have some ideas that are new to you, and they may come as a big surprise.

Compromise has been the key to more than a few political careers and good marriages, not to mention a few billion working relationships of all kinds. But compromising and giving in are not the same thing.

Compromise implies movement, a movement by both sides of an issue toward a middle ground. In the case of an architect who has presented you with a possibility you simply don't like, you can of course take a tough position and say, "No, it isn't acceptable, change it." You're the person with the checkbook, you've got to live in the place, so make up your own mind.

On the other hand, you have hired the architect to help you. He can do so in a number of different ways, but only if you let him.

Hear him out. Consider carefully what he is saying. He may give you a series of design arguments that don't make sense to you, using words like "proportion" and "balance." He may also be thinking of your pocketbook: small-seeming changes can significantly affect prices. Listen first, then make up your mind.

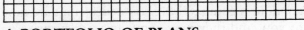

A PORTFOLIO OF PLANS

The building department and other agencies in your community will require a variety of documents before issuing your building permit. (Your bank probably will, too.) Requirements vary from state to state and city to city, but the basic ingredients of the plan package are those described on the following pages.

The working drawings are done to scale on tracing paper. When copied, they are called blueprints because the traditional method of reproduction resulted in a print of white lines on a blue background. These days the drawings are more often produced by a copying machine in black and white and can be reduced to smaller sheets for easy reference on standard copiers. In fact, it is is a good idea to have small sets made to keep in your files for reference.

The drawings that follow are for a one-family home in suburban New Jersey. The house is an appealing blend of the Victorian styling of its neighbors and of contemporary indoor/outdoor spaces. These drawings are simplified from the original design by Richard Bennett of Loeffler, Johansen, Bennett of New York.

THE PLOT PLAN

The architect or designer will execute this and the rest of the drawings for you. If, however, you are using stock plans, you will have to hire a local surveyor to draw this one for you.

The scale of a plot plan is commonly $\frac{1}{16}''$ or $\frac{1}{8}''$ per foot.

The plot plan is just what the name suggests: it is a plan of the plot on which your house is or will be located. The boundaries of the property are indicated, as is the foundation

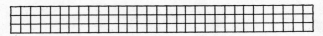

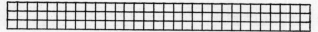

of the house. In addition, any zoning or other restrictions will be drawn in, including setbacks and easements. Necessary site work, utilities, and the vistas that will be visible from the house should also be indicated.

A plot plan isn't necessary if you are simply finishing off existing space in your house, but for an addition or a completely new building, one will be required.

A plot plan is also sometimes referred to as a "plat" plan, though more properly a plat plan is a map or plan of a larger area that indicates the locations and boundaries of individual properties. Another name sometimes used is "site" plan.

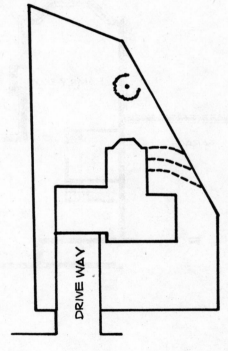

DRIVE WAY

KATHERINE STREET

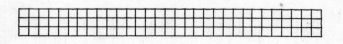

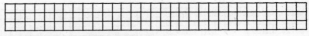

FOUNDATION PLAN

The foundation plan shows the outside dimensions of the house. It will be used by the subcontractors who do the grading and excavation of the property and those who install the footings and build the foundation walls.

The foundation plan will indicate the required dimensions of the footings and walls, the location of basement windows, plumbing, and doors (if any), of load-bearing elements (piers and reinforcing rods, for example), and of any other constituent parts of the foundation.

The scale is usually ⅛″ per foot.

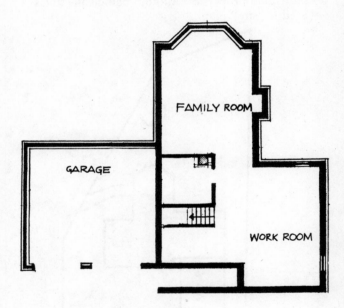

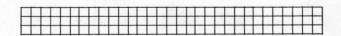

FLOOR PLANS

The floor plans indicate inside and outside walls, the openings in them (windows and doors), appliances, and plumbing fixtures.

A floor plan shows a horizontal section of the house. That is, it shows what you would see if you were to slice through the walls at one height and look down on the truncated structure from above. Although the final working plans will not incorporate key pieces of furniture, early drafts should indicate them.

There will be a floor plan for each floor of the house, and there may also be a floor plan for each of the mechanical tradesmen (the plumber, electrician, and heating, ventilation, and air-conditioning, or HVAC, contractor). On the electrical plan, for example, the location of the electrical panel, the meter, and other elements of the system will be indicated. The more complex the job, the more electrical, plumbing, and mechanical plans there will be. On a small job, all the wiring and plumbing and the rest may be combined onto a single sheet.

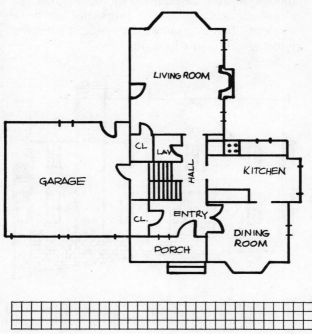

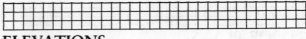

ELEVATIONS

The plot, foundation, and floor plans are all top views, schematic drawings made from the vantage of a bird flying directly overhead.

Elevations show views of the completed exterior or interior of a building. The point of view is that of an observer looking straight at the wall. However, elevations are two-dimensional drawings and have no perspective, though, in some cases, there will be shading. The elevations indicate patterns, proportions, and materials, but do no more than suggest what the building will finally look like.

The number and variety of elevations you need will vary depending upon the design. For example, you would need no interior elevations for an entirely new house if it is to be finished throughout with standard drywall and stock appliances and cabinets. On the other hand, the renovation of a single room with complex paneling or moldings might require an elevation drawing of each wall of the room.

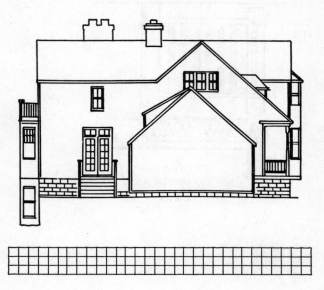

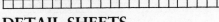

DETAIL SHEETS

Accompanying the elevations will be details and sectional drawings. These are illustrations that explain to the builder features that will be specially constructed. Cabinetry, unusual interior moldings or design elements, and numerous other aspects that require special information for construction or assembly are likely to be featured in details or sections.

The detail sheets will provide your subcontractors with guidance for the details of the finish, everything from the shape and dimension of the cornice molding to the kitchen cabinets. A detail sheet specifies the materials that make up the walls (of both the house and the foundation).

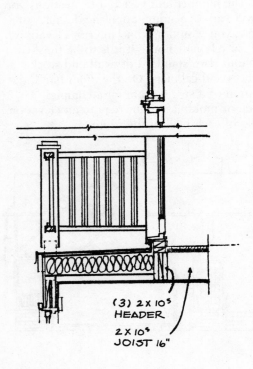

(3) 2 X 10^s
HEADER

2 X 10^s
JOIST 16"

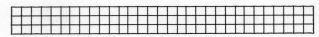

SPECIFICATIONS

The finished plans will be accompanied by a series of specification sheets. The first pages of specs are essentially the standards for the performance of the work outlined in the finished drawings. The subjects covered will include time schedule, quality of acceptable workmanship, insurance requirements, working conditions, and installation requirements for equipment.

These pages will be accompanied by schedules that list the kinds of doors, windows, hardware, and other finishes. Each working drawing for specific trades, including the ones for the electrician and the plumber, for example, will have its own spec sheet.

Spec sheets don't have to be infinitely detailed—in fact, if they are some builders and subcontractors will be hesitant to bid—but particularly with appliances, windows and doors, special-order materials, and fixtures, brand names and numbers and other details such as color and size should be specified.

SECTION 08600 - WOOD DOORS AND WINDOWS

PART 1 GENERAL

1.01   Work Included: The Contractor shall provide all
        labor materials, equipment and accessories, and
        perform all operations in connection with doors
        and windows, including but not limited to the
        following:
   A. Wood terrace doors and entry door in rough
        openings.

   B. Wood windows in rough   openings.

   C. Wood interior doors and door frames.

1.02   Quality Assurance: All items shall conform to
        National Woodworkers Manufacturers Association
        applicable standards.

PART 2 PRODUCTS

2.01   EXTERIOR WOOR AND GLASS TERRACE DOORS: shall be
        as manufactured by Marvin Windows, Warroad,
        Minnesota 56763, telephone 218-386-1430.

2.02   ENTRANCE DOOR: shall be a 1 3/4 inch thick
        exterior door type M-7135 as manufactured by
        Morgan Door Products Oshkosh, Wisconsin. (800)
        435-7464.

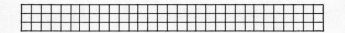

MORE PRELIMINARY ESTIMATES. In Chapter 1 we talked about quickie, per-square-foot estimates. Now, if you have hired an architect or designer, that person, as part of his professional services, will provide some ballpark estimates.

Frank Lloyd Wright was once asked if he could design a $10,000 house. That was more than fifty years ago, so the question wasn't so outrageous as it sounds today.

His reply was to the point. He said he could, but added that he could not design a $20,000 house for $10,000.

There is a simple formula to keep in mind as you think about the estimated cost of your house, especially if you are concerned with cutting dollars out of it. It is this:

BUDGET = Quality of Materials × Size

It's deceivingly simple but it's practically a law of nature. If you want to bring down the price, you will have to shrink the house or compromise on some of the materials. True, there are other extraordinary options that we will discuss later (being your own contractor, for example, is the subject of a later chapter), but in general this formula is painfully accurate.

The Last Word There's only one thing to keep in mind when you are buying services, whether it's having a flat tire fixed by a grease monkey or surgery performed by the most prestigious surgeon you can find.

It's an easy one to remember: The only stupid question is the unasked question.

It's your money you are spending, so make sure you understand what you are getting, and that what you are getting is what you want. You sign the checks, so get all your questions answered first, then pay the bill.

3

LABOR AND MATERIALS

Manning and Estimating

Once you have a design, it's time to turn it into a building. This chapter is about how to do that: by buying the best materials and services at the best possible price. By necessity, this chapter also involves more than a little discussion of how to manage those services.

As with any other management task, it is important to understand the different roles played by the different players, and in home construction they are certainly diverse. If you use a designer or architect to put your dreams on paper, then the people you meet later in the actual construction process will seem like a breed apart from the designer.

My first experience with tradesmen came in high school when I spent a summer working as an electrician's assistant in a furniture factory in New England. I handed tools to the head electrician as he tried to keep a lot of outdated machinery functioning two shifts a day.

His job also involved "special projects." One of the vice-presidents of the company was an electrical engineer, and he would occasionally draw up plans for new machines, which he would then ask my boss and others in the shop to execute.

No doubt the VP was a good engineer. I am equally confident that my boss was an experienced and capable electrician. But, strangely, they didn't seem to speak anything like the same language. The VP knew his theories, and he could write formulas and draw perfect plans. The electrician was a hands-on man who could fix anything, and he had a detective's talent for following the smallest clue through to the solution. As compatible as these skills would seem to be, in practice there was more conflict than coordination.

When one of these new designs would arrive, my boss would shake his head sadly. He would eventually get around to looking closely at the plans, his face alternately smiling and frowning. Occasionally a chuckle would be heard. I remember one time when the plans ended up on the floor with him jumping up and down on them.

The problem was that the VP would often put on paper the impossible. You just cannot fit square pegs into round holes, but if the pegs and holes are simply abstract numbers and symbols on your drafting board, then you have no way of knowing you are creating unreality. On the other hand, if your world is as concrete and specific as your last order of wire from the electrical supplier, then it is incomprehensible to you how any highfalutin engineer type could be so dumb as to put such silliness on paper.

The upshot was always that my boss translated the plan, changing this component and rearranging that aspect of the design. He built the machines, and sometimes they worked very well, sometimes they were a waste of time and money. The VP and the electrician eventually came to like one another, and taught each other quite a few things. But they never saw the world in the same way.

The odds are that your architect and your general contractor will be a similar match-up. The architect thinks and theorizes and draws; the contractor wields his hammer to turn the paper drawings into three-dimensional structures. They inevitably spend some of their time resenting each other. And then they get the job done.

Managing your renovation or construction project involves more than handling different sorts of people. To make it sound a good deal simpler than it is, good management really is a matter of good decisions, no more, no less. Some decisions have to do with money matters, others with personnel.

Any manager—whether it's a construction manager or a toy company president—will tell you that the key to making a decision is having the right information available. If you have done your homework and assembled the hard information like the estimates and the schedules, and also have collected the softer data like reputations and the sometimes contradictory advice and guidance of friends and family, and weighed in your own feelings and considerations, you are in a position to make good decisions.

In fact, you may be surprised at how many decisions are made for you by state and local codes. The expertise of your principal advisers—once you decide who they will be—will help you. The architect's training has taught him about such things as the strength of materials, while the carpenter has had to face many of the same problems before.

When it comes to making decisions, don't labor too long over them. As any good manager will tell you, no decision should require more time to make than it takes to collect the relevant information. So learn what you need to know, listen to your advisers, and make reasoned and prompt decisions.

If you find yourself second-guessing yourself, that's no crime. Don't be afraid to admit you made a mistake, but correct it immediately upon realizing it. Consider this instance: In re-modeling the foyer to their apartment, David and Andrea selected mauve tile. Judging from one piece of tile, they thought it was magnificent. But when the tile arrived, they excitedly spread it on the floor to get a sense of the overall effect, and the color was simply overpowering. In David's words: "It just didn't work. We called the tile store the next morning, switched to a bluish gray, and paid a 35 percent restocking charge." He concludes of the decision: "It was a small price to pay under the circumstances."

Assembling the Crew

One basic assumption of this book is that you are the manager, that you will be hiring people to build your house for you. Depending on whether you arrange to supervise the work yourself or have an architect or general contractor do it, you will have more or less responsibility to be on top of things.

Do you want your architect to run the construction portion of the job for you? There are arguments both pro and con. The arguments in favor are that your architect will save you time. If he's minding the store, you don't have to. Also, he knows whom to call to get quotes on a job, whereas you would most likely have to do some research and waste some time following up worthless leads. His job is to know who does the kind of construction work you need and who is ill suited to the job.

He may also be able to get services and attention you would not, since he can offer contractors consideration for future jobs, whereas you are unlikely to be embarking on another project for a while. His business is soliciting and reviewing bids, so he knows what to look for. He has also spent many, many hours resolving disagreements. They are inevitable, and he can help.

He knows the contracts. He can help you make the best decisions regarding materials. He knows building and zoning codes. He can inspect along the way (remember, his job is not to supervise, as the contractors do that; his job is to inspect what's been done, approve or disapprove, and advise you when payment is due). He can help decide on the inevitable small changes that occur in the course of construction. He can serve as a valuable buffer between you and the contractor. For this, you pay him an agreed-upon additional percentage of the construction cost.

An alternative is leaving the supervision to the general contractor, whom we will meet shortly, or being your own general contractor (see Chapter 4). But whatever you do, you need to know who the players are in the game you are about to play. In Chapter 2 you were introduced to the designer/architect; now it's time to meet the crew.

The General Contractor These days, most home construction is done under the guidance of a general contractor, or GC, often a carpenter by trade. The general contractor's responsibility is to devise, supervise, and adapt the overall battle plan.

The general contractor will take your plans and build your house. It is really that simple: he is responsible for the whole process. You sign a contract with him and you pay him at certain specified points, but he handles the rest of it. (See Chapter 5 for discussion of contracts and payments.)

Most states and municipalities require that general contractors be licensed. But whether they are licensed or not, their job is to arrange for all the subcontractors—the plumbers and electricians and the rest—and to make sure they do their jobs on time and in strict accordance with the plans. The GC makes his money by marking up the labor and materials costs by a percentage. That percentage varies considerably. The typical range is 10 to 30 percent.

There are several kinds of contractors. Many are veteran carpenters who decided they could run the whole show themselves, so they became managers. Others are companies rather than individuals. In the case of the carpenter-builder, he probably has only one job (perhaps two) going at any one time, while a construction company is likely to require more jobs to pay its overhead. The carpenter-builder probably doesn't have an office and a payroll clerk and the other accoutrements of a good-sized business, whereas the construction company will.

Each has its advantages. The carpenter-builder is more likely to be a craftsman who enjoys his trade, and developing a flexible working relationship with a carpenter-builder is easier than with a company. On the other hand, the construction company probably has a much greater capacity. If your project is very large (3,000 square feet or more) you will benefit from the larger crews of a construction company.

It isn't always true that the construction company has to charge more to pay for the extra overhead costs, as there are some economies of scale. But in general the chances are good that as a small, one-time buyer of construction services, you'll do better with a carpenter-builder. He is probably more accustomed to dealing with individual owners, he no doubt will have more time for your special concerns, and he may well price the job a little cheaper, too. If you're in doubt, get both companies and carpenter-builders to bid on your job (see "Estimating," later in this chapter).

How do you tell the difference? Ask the general contractors you talk to how many jobs they have going at any one time. If the man you talk to is dressed in a business suit, chances are he will be going back to an office; if the GC tells you about eleven other ongoing jobs, he's running a big outfit.

Another concern in selecting a GC is experience. If your general contractor is a carpenter just branching out and trying his hand at being a carpenter-builder, beware. He may take to his profession quickly and be wonderful at it, but it is a new profession for him, one requiring a lot less hand-eye coordination and a good deal more business sense. Be a guinea pig if you like. It may work out to your advantage, as many people embarking upon a new career have a pride in accomplishment that will have faded by the time the umpteenth job rolls around. But make sure you are confident he has the scheduling, budgeting, and other skills to assume his expanded duties.

The process of hiring a GC is not radically different from that of hiring an architect. You want to hire someone with proven skills, somebody you can work with, and someone with a sound business sense for schedules and hiring capable help. If your architect is staying with you through construction, he handles the hiring of the GC for you.

If you are on your own and you don't know where to begin, ask friends or acquaintances who have had home construction done for their recommendations. Personal references are always best. Personal to you, that is, not to the contractor. As long as the contractor isn't a favored nephew the referrer is trying to help out, the chances are you'll get a fair assessment of a contractor's skills. Moreover, you can examine his finished work. That's one reason why you will usually do best hiring a local contractor with an established business.

Ask the customer if the finished work was acceptable. Did the contractor finish at or near the budgeted price? If not, were the change orders reasonable? Was the work completed on schedule? Did the contractor willingly return to correct problems? Would they use him again?

Another source of contractors is your local lumberyard(s). Not houseware stores where nails are sold by the dozen, but real building supply houses where contractors do their bulk business. The proprietors of such places know who the reliable contractors are. They know which contractors pay their bills on time, whose orders are always confused, and which ones are always returning merchandise.

It is perfectly acceptable (indeed, it is necessary) to ask each GC you interview for four or five local references. Once you have them, check them out. Call the customers, identify yourself as a homeowner in the market for building services, and ask whether his or her job was done on time, whether the completed job was satisfactory, if the price changed along the way, if the workers were neat or left a hopeless mess behind. Ask to drop by and have a look at the work. Only by comparing it yourself to what you know and like can you make a good judgment about the caliber and acceptability of a contractor's work.

Just to be safe, call the the local Better Business Bureau and ask if they have any complaints on file against the contractor(s) you are thinking of hiring. You might also check at the local building department. Ask each contractor who his primary supplier of materials is, and then call that supplier.

A call to a local credit bureau is also a good idea. Ask how long the company has been in business. If you uncover any pending suits or liens, walk away. You don't need the problems that can occur when a contractor is in litigation, like the sheriff arriving to impound the contractor's tools—or your building supplies.

Other sources for references are banks and subcontractors. Ask the GC whom he has dealt with and call them, too. The banks can tell you about his financial responsibility and the subcontractors about how well organized he is.

OTHER OPTIONS. A "construction manager" is an alternative to the traditional general contractor. The principal difference is economic: instead of the GC calculating his costs and then marking them up a percentage to give you one price, the construction manager will simply be paid a percentage of the costs as a professional fee. You pay your suppliers, subs, and other creditors directly. (With a general contractor all your construction payments are to the contractor, who, in turn, pays the materials, subcontractor, and other bills.)

Your architect may be willing to be your construction manager, and some general contractors will work on a manager-fee basis. But whoever does it, the estimating, negotiations, scheduling, and supervision are the manager's responsibility. Fees vary, but generally they are less than 15 percent. There are also standard contracts available (including one from the American Institute of Architects) to guide this relationship.

Whatever arrangement you decide upon, remember that you're the boss. Insist that the work be up to your standards.

The Subcontractors The subcontractors are so called because of their relationship to the general contractor. Each sub will work for the GC (or, in some cases, the architect or you yourself), and will be responsible for completing a specified task or tasks for a specified price.

Depending on the nature of your construction, you may require a number of subcontractors or none. Among the subs required for new residential construction are a surveyor, an earth-moving subcontractor for excavation and site preparation, a concrete contractor for the foundation footings (he may also build the cellar walls if they are to be of block, though another sub, a mason, may be required). Electrical, plumbing, and HVAC (heating, ventilation, and air conditioning) contractors may be necessary and, depending upon who your GC or carpenter is, roofing, drywall, painting, and cleanup contractors may be required, too. Usually any vinyl flooring, tile, and Formica jobs can be done by one contractor, while another will sell and install your carpeting. If there is landscaping to be done, still another sub may be necessary. Depending on local and state requirements, at least the electrician, plumber, and surveyor will be required to be licensed.

If you have a general contractor handling your job, he'll be in charge of hiring, scheduling, paying, and supervising the subs. (If you are hiring them yourself, see Chapter 4.)

Each sub should be responsible for any inspections your community requires. The plumber should arrange for the plumbing inspection, the electrician for the wiring check, and so on.

We will talk about this at some length in the next chapter when we deal with contracts, but keep in mind that you should pay only for completed work. And you should pay only for work that is correctly completed. Once you've paid your bill, there's no incentive for a sub to return and fix the problem. So make sure it's right before writing the check.

If your job is a small renovation and you opt to hire, say, the carpenter and electrician yourself, their hiring is no different from the hiring of a GC or an architect. You want someone able to do the job who will get along with the other workers and who will adhere to deadlines.

Again, ask suppliers for recommendations. Check out references. After you make a couple of calls or visits, you'll begin to get a pretty clear sense of the subs and how people feel about them. And while you're talking to the references, ask them about suppliers or subs who they felt did especially good work or whom they think highly of. Another method of finding subs is to visit job sites: if you see a house under construction, wander in and ask for the boss. Often in the case of subs, the chief is on site, and may even be able to give you an estimate then and there.

All subs must carry insurance. Ask them for a copy of their Certificate of Insurance.

Another word to the wise: Don't get too friendly with any of your contractors. Keep your relationships strictly professional. They aren't your friends; they are people with whom you have a business relationship. Be their buddy later, after the job is done.

Sources of Supplies

There is no right or wrong way to go about buying the materials you need. An argument can be made for going the supermarket route and buying most or all of your materials from one large supplier. There is also a reasonable counter-argument for going from the butcher to the baker to the candlestick maker and shopping for the best deals.

If you hire a general contractor, he will resolve this problem for you. You are paying him to manage the whole process, including the ordering, the delivery schedule, and the other hassles attendant upon getting the right materials at the right price. But if you are managing this aspect of the job, then pay close attention.

In the case of new construction, one way or another you'll need to tap sources for some of the following:

Sand and gravel may be needed for foundation work.

Concrete block, brick, or concrete almost certainly will be required.

Lumber: Your source of lumber will stock framing lumber, nails and other fasteners, roofing and siding materials, and interior and exterior trim. Depending on which lumber supplier you choose and the nature of your project, you may also buy windows and doors, light fixtures, drywall, cabinets, and insulation from the lumber company.

However, if you don't go for the supermarket approach, you may make contact with one or another of the following: a millwork shop for windows, doors, elaborate paneling or other woodwork that has been finished, machined, and assembled at the mill; a lighting fixture supply house; a drywall supplier for the gypsum board, joint compound, and other supplies needed for hanging the plaster-like sheets; an insulation supplier (often also a contractor), who will provide and install foam or other insulation requiring specialized equipment and expertise.

Buying from the smaller supplier may save money, as the larger lumber company will add a markup to the price they pay, so if you can get the same trade discount from the original supplier, you won't have to pay the extra percentage.

If you do end up ordering supplies, be sure to consult often with your GC or subs about delivery. You don't want to have materials piled at the work site waiting to be used, since the

THE THREE D'S OF SUPPLIER BUYING

DISCOUNTS: Be sure to ask your suppliers for the builder's discount. You are a builder, so you should act like one and get the benefits. Your suppliers are unlikely to complain—after all, you are not asking for anything more than many of the suppliers' other customers get. However, if your project is a relatively small renovation, don't be surprised if the answer is no. Some suppliers have monthly minimums for qualifying for builder's discounts (typically, a thousand dollars or more), so if they tell you no, the preferred builder's terms are not available to you, ask why not and what the required qualifications are.

DELIVERY: Many suppliers will deliver at no charge. Make sure to establish that they do, and if not, what the charges will be. If there is a delivery fee, shop around a bit to see what other suppliers do. Also, beware of "sidewalk delivery." A familiar concept to apartment dwellers, it means that that five-hundred-pound appliance will be delivered to the sidewalk—even if your apartment is on the tenth floor.

DOLLAR DAYS: Most suppliers will want to check your credit (they will want to know the bank from which you've gotten your loan and/or several other credit references). Having established that you are not a deadbeat, most suppliers will offer at least thirty-day terms in which to pay. Goods that arrive this month won't have to be paid for until next.

Find out exactly what each supplier's terms are, as some suppliers offer a 1½ or 2 percent discount for speedy payments.

sooner you get them, the sooner you have to pay for them. Also, stacks of goods are very inviting to thieves. In the parlance of the business, they have a tendency to "walk away."

You must also be sure to check with suppliers about availability. Find out when you have to order that special tile and odd-size window in order to have them available when they are needed. Cabinets and heating equipment are most likely to require the longest order time, and their absence can slow down the job.

Estimating

When you pay your taxes, you have two choices, the long form and the short form. Both have applications; both are the "right" way in certain instances.

In estimating the cost of your new house or your renovation, you face a similar choice. The simple way is to use average square-foot costs, spelled out in Chapter 1; the more complex way is to get actual estimates for the labor and materials needed.

The square-foot averages are especially useful if you are building an entirely new house of a familiar design that uses stock materials. On the other hand, if you plan to buy custom doors and try to match the old moldings from Grandma's eighteenth-century house, the averages are going to be of little help. And remodeling inevitably defies the standard numbers provided by per-square-foot cost tables.

For most new-house projects, however, the averages will be helpful in the early stages for establishing ballpark estimates. If the estimate you reach using averages comes to twice the money you have to spend, you know you have to rethink the project and you haven't wasted lots of the designer's, suppliers', and your own time.

Once you are confident that you like the design, it is time to get takeoffs for the materials. (A takeoff is the list of materials required for a particular job, usually derived from the architect's specification sheets.) Be as comfortable as possible with the design, however, before doing so. Changes can be made anytime you want, but the later in the process they come and the bigger they are, the more expensive they become. Virtually no changes come for free.

As the sample plans in Chapter 2 suggest, specification sheets are a part of the basic plan, whether it is a stock plan or a tailor-made design fresh from the drawing board. Spec sheets should spell out the needed materials in as much detail as possible, citing everything from the brand name and model number of the kitchen appliances to the thickness and quality of the plywood to be used for subflooring.

Spec sheets will often specify the decorative items, too, such as doorknobs and paint and moldings. There you are likely to be introduced to the term "or equal." Also called "allowances," "or equal" materials are usually finish materials like carpeting or floor tiles or hardware. Here, if you don't like any of the items listed on the spec sheets, you may substitute for them, with the contractor's agreement, at no extra cost if your new choice costs the same as what was specified. However, it probably won't come as a great surprise to you that generally the allowances specified in the estimates are not for top-of-the-line goods. So if your substitute costs more, the cost goes up. (Remember, changes should be made now, not tomorrow. If one of your subs has ordered the materials specified, then you own them. He may agree to buy them back from you, but chances are he'll only be willing to pay fifty cents or so on the dollar.)

Once again, if you have a general contractor acting on your behalf, he will handle the estimating. He will give you one price for the whole job and you will negotiate with him. However, if you are responsible for dealing with the suppliers and subcontractors, you will have to review individual bids.

The plans and the spec sheets are all you need to solicit bids. They will be divided by trades

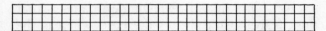

ESTIMATING HINTS

Get at least three estimates for each job, whether it's the whole job or only one subcontractor's portion of it. Only when you have a basis for comparison will the outrageously expensive estimate stand out. And remember, the cheapest isn't always the best. If one price is much less than the others, there's probably a reason why.

Get your job estimated during the off-season. This won't help in Southern California, where construction work isn't seasonal, but in the snow belt you may well get a better number from a contractor during the idle months when he wants to line up work for the first day of spring. Even if a contractor's prices don't vary much from season to season, he'll almost surely have more time to devote to working out the estimate carefully and maybe even to helping you brainstorm about costs and technical concerns.

so that the carpenter, electrician, plumber, and the rest will be able to estimate the labor and materials required to complete their parts of the job. You give them the paperwork they need, and they will respond in kind, providing you with written estimates of what they will do for how much. As we will see in Chapter 5, these estimates often become a part of the contract between you and the contractors, but for now our concern is with determining which estimate is best.

The key in reviewing estimates—and you should solicit three or more for each task—is to be sure all are comparable. Read them carefully. They should have been done on the basis of the same specifications, but occasionally a tradesman will substitute for this or that item. It may be an improvement, it may save you money or it may not, but be sure you know what has been changed. The estimate should refer specifically to the specs, perhaps in lawyer-style language like "This estimate prepared per specifications and plans submitted by Client and attached hereto . . ."

Let's consider a takeoff estimate done by a lumber supplier, for example, for a deck you are adding to your house. You are using a plan you found advertised in a home design magazine, and it comes complete with a spec sheet that lists the lumber, nails, and other materials needed. You hand the list to the clerk at your lumberyard and ask him to have an estimate prepared. Usually, they will provide this service at no charge. You will then be given a written estimate with the price, payment schedule, and other terms specified.

As a general rule, the three or four estimates you get for a particular job will be in the same range, plus or minus 10 percent of the middle figure. However, if one is very high, that suggests the contractor doesn't want the job. Be happy for him; it means he's got plenty of work.

One rule of reviewing estimates is that the cheapest isn't always the best, whereas the most expensive isn't always best either. If one estimate is very low, it isn't necessarily happy days for you. Check that estimate out very carefully. The contractor may not have understood the job, or may have specified cheaper materials or changed something important. Don't just sign on the dotted line in order to save yourself that money. In the end, it may not be a saving at all.

Compare the estimates you get with the projections your architect provided. It is unreasonable to expect that his numbers will match up exactly with the estimates, but he should be in the same range with most of them unless specifications have been changed significantly. If none of your estimates are in the range the architect said they should be, meet with him and try to find out why. Even if it is merely a matter of his making a mistake, he should know about it. And he just may point to something that the estimators missed that accounts for the discrepancy.

Other Concerns

Building Codes and Permits The earliest known building code came into existence in Babylon some eighteen centuries before the birth of Christ. Roughly translated, that code read in part: "If a builder has built a house for a man and his work is not strong, and if the house he has built falls in and kills the householder, that builder shall be slain."

Although such a penalty probably exceeds the expectations of even the most militant consumer advocate, the basic intent of today's building code is essentially the same: Build it right, Buster, or else.

THE BUILDING CODE. The building code in your area is likely to be one of the three "standard" codes. One is called the "Uniform Building Code" and is published by the International Conference of Building Officials; the others have similar names and very similar contents. You should be able to get a copy of the building code for your area—or find out where to get one—at the local building department at City Hall. The yellow pages is another good place to find out where to get one. If you don't succeed at either, try the reference librarian at your local library.

You don't have to read the code from cover to cover. Your architect or general contractor and each of the subcontractors are responsible for meeting code standards for plumbing, electrical, and the rest. Nevertheless, it isn't a bad idea to have a general sense of what the code is, and, specifically, to be familiar with any general guidance offered in the volume's opening pages. If your community has issued its own supplementary guidelines, be sure you read those, especially if one or more of your contractors do not customarily do work in your town or city. There may be special considerations you wish to bring to their attention. It is their job to know, but a little reminder from you won't hurt.

Building codes vary, but the issues addressed in all of them include structural strength, standards for materials for the working systems (wire sizes, gauge of pipe), and other matters for which your contractors will be responsible. Other issues your architect/designer will have to be aware of are minimum sizes for rooms, fenestration (windows), ceiling heights, and fire exits.

In general, building codes are long, complicated volumes. If you were to take it upon yourself to learn all of the regulations, it would be a lot like going back to school for another degree. It isn't necessary to know it all, but you may wish to have a sense of what's there.

THE BUILDING PERMIT. Find out what the requirements are for a building permit. The codes will tell you what you need to do to get a "certificate of occupancy" ("C. of O."), but even before you break ground you'll need a permit.

In order to get a permit, you will have to have plans and specifications for the project; many states and municipalities require that the drawings bear the stamp of a licensed architect or engineer. If your project is new construction, then you will probably be required to provide engineering reports as well. Ask your local building inspector if such reports are required.

Due dates are particularly important in applying for a building permit. If, for example, you are constructing a new home in an area where municipal sewage treatment is not available, you will probably have to contend with a stringent array of tests and timetables. The ability of the property to absorb water (and waste materials) will have to be tested. In some parts of the country, a percolation test can only be done at certain times of the year, so if you miss the cutoff date, you might have to delay construction an entire year. Find out what the dates and limitations are.

You may discover that your contractor or architect automatically assumes responsibility for getting the required permits. However, if the task falls to you, be aware that in some communities separate permits are required for electrical, plumbing, and other building tasks. Your local building department can tell you what is necessary. When it comes time to file, ask what paperwork they require but anticipate that you will have to provide them with at least one set of the plans, along with your address, a general description of the work to be done and its approximate cost, and an explanation of what the space will be used for. The cost estimate is necessary because the fees in many areas are determined on the basis of a sliding scale depending upon the cost or size of the construction.

INSPECTIONS. The local building code or building inspector can provide you with details about what inspections are necessary, but typically inspections are required of new foundations, at the completion of the rough framing, after the plumbing and electrical services have been "roughed in," of the electrical and plumbing after completion, and perhaps even of the insulation. Some communities require more, some less, but usually before the certificate of occupancy is issued the inspections must be complete. The nature of the job is also a determining factor; obviously, if your project involves no plumbing work, then no plumbing inspections will be required.

The Last Word

INSURANCE. When you hire your GC, subs, and other on-site workers, inquire whether each has insurance. They should have a blanket policy that covers them in the event of personal or property loss. You don't want to pay for a laborer's hospitalization for a broken leg or his workman's compensation.

Ask each contractor to provide you with a copy of his certificate of insurance along with his estimate. If he balks, get another contractor.

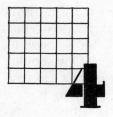

4

How to Be Your Own Contractor

For most people, attempting to be one's own architect is a bad idea—for all the reasons discussed in Chapter 2. On the other hand, there is no mystery to being a general contractor.

Some skills with people and finances and general good sense are required. For someone who has never done it, a willingness to ask questions, some of which may seem silly or ignorant, is necessary. And a certain knack for solving problems is certainly helpful.

The single most significant argument for trying to be your own contractor is that the payoff can be considerable. After all, contractors write a substantial profit and overhead margin into every job; it varies, but 20 percent is usual. If you are your own GC, you won't have to pay anyone that percentage.

All of this is not to say that you should be your own contractor. That's a decision you have to make yourself on the basis of your available time, your inclinations, and your need or desire to save some dollars.

Being your own contractor does not mean wielding a hammer all day. Most emphatically not, in fact, as the only tools you will require are a pair of tape measures. One should be long (a 50- or 100-footer), the other a shorter, belt-hanger model at least 16 feet in length.

Being your own contractor often means that you increase the odds of getting exactly what you want. The professional GCs do their job simply and efficiently so that it gets done quickly and they can get on to the next job. Changes along the way and variations from the usual make the job last longer and can be the cause of irritation and uncooperativeness on the part of a GC. So if you are very detail-conscious and plan to be looking over everybody's shoulder anyway, it may make sense for you to be your own GC.

Many states and municipalities require that general contractors be licensed and properly insured before they can legally hang out a shingle identifying themselves as GCs. However, no such requirements exist for the homeowner acting as his own GC. If after you do it yourself you like it so much you want to do it again for someone else, find out what the requirements are.

To Be or Not to Be

There are happy stories and horror stories about people who decide to be their own contractors. Here's one of each.

Madeline's husband, Roger, was about to launch his own medical practice in a picturesque Connecticut shore town. They bought a fifty-year-old house and set about converting it into an office and home.

They knew what they wanted and decided against the expense of hiring a professional designer. Roger drew a floor plan to scale indicating the changes and adjustments to be made. They found a reputable carpenter-builder in the area and negotiated a cost-plus agreement for the work.

Roger was still seeing patients in their

old town (they couldn't afford the down time while they waited for the house and office space to be finished), so they were still living fifty miles away when the work got underway. They planned to move in when the work was completed.

Two weeks into the job, they drove down on a Saturday to inspect the progress. They didn't like what they found. Not only did the progress seem slow, but a new partition was being constructed in the wrong place and a number of smaller problems were immediately evident.

Always the sort who willingly takes the bull by the horns, Madeline decided on the spot that an on-site supervisor was necessary. She moved in the next weekend, against the advice of almost everyone involved.

For almost two months Madeline was without a working shower or bath. The kitchen was out of commission for days at a time. Plaster dust clung to her like dandruff, and the builders got to see how firm she could be as well as how charming. And she got the job she wanted, down to the last detail.

The lesson Madeline and Roger learned was that if you don't have every last detail of the plans down on paper, you've got to be there. Their course of action isn't for everyone, but it is an option, especially if the absence of detailed plans requires decisions practically every hour. No matter how detailed the plans, however, the GC must be reachable, at least by telephone, throughout the working day. Indecision usually means delay, and delays generally mean money.

Madeline and Roger got the job done well, on budget, and on time. And the savings that resulted from not having to pay the GC's percentage made it possible: they had to stretch to do the job. Now, Roger's practice is growing rapidly, and Madeline is beginning to think about what kind of house she would like to buy as a permanent home, and just how it might be adapted.

The other side of the argument is Dan

Mandino, a restaurateur. He ran a small lunch place in Boston's North End for several years and built a profitable business before losing his lease. He found a new space a few blocks south on the chic waterfront and prepared to start again.

A major renovation was necessary. The space had been a restaurant, but it had closed years before and had remained shuttered ever since. To put it charitably, the place was a mess. The kitchen had to be completely gutted because the roof had severe leaks, and the appliances were rusted beyond usefulness. The dining area was just as bad, mostly because of the original decor, a very dated-looking Mediterranean style with imitation hand-hewn wood members and tattered leatherette.

Danny decided to be his own GC. First he hired a carpenter, a regular customer at his previous establishment. The carpenter referred an electrician, and the electrician a plumber. A plasterer came next. The personnel gradually got hired and it seemed as if the job was progressing.

Like Madeline, Danny decided to be a constant, on-site presence. After all, he had no restaurant to run until the new one was finished, so he figured another laborer on the premises could only speed things up.

He worked with the carpenter and some of the other tradesmen. He helped here and there. He developed some skills himself. He was there for every step in the process and had the opportunity to see his dream emerge—one tiny step at a time—before his very eyes.

He freely admits that he never wanted to be a tradesman or a contractor. His life is food and drink, not hammers and nails. He didn't get a better job just because he was there to oversee everything, since his architect came almost daily and inspected and invariably came up with numerous changes Danny had not noticed a need for.

Perhaps even more important, he cost himself months. Instead of delegating responsibility for the small decisions to his subs, he got involved in discussions of the minutest details, and his inexperience led to a multitude of scheduling problems. Sometimes work had to be done twice. The electrician was there but the carpenter wasn't, so wire went in temporarily and then had to be partially taken out. Then the carpenter did his work and the wires got put back later.

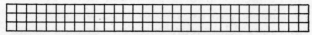

DO YOU REALLY WANT TO BE YOUR OWN CONTRACTOR?

Before deciding whether to be your own GC, ask yourself if you have the following:

THE TIME. True, it won't take all day. In fact, rarely should you have to invest more than two hours a day and only during construction should it take that long. But you do have to be available for emergencies. Some general contractors are so confident in their subs they rarely even go to the job site, but don't count on being able to do this, especially the first time around. Can you make the trek to the job at lunch hours and after work and attend to other details by phone?

THE PERSONALITY. Yes, you'll have to be tough at times with your subs. But equally important, you can't be forever interfering with their work. Can you be a manager with the confidence to let the pros do the work they know how to do better than you and the instinct to know when to step in?

THE INCLINATION. This isn't a task to be assumed lightly. You can't just hand it off to someone else halfway through. It's start to finish, with no turning back.

THE MONEY. You will be required to spend some of your own money while you are waiting for the bank to come through with the payments. All general contractors have to do the same thing, paying their men and buying supplies. Do you have the capital to do it?

The job got done. The restaurant looks wonderful and, to judge by the crowds at dinnertime, the consensus is that the food and atmosphere are good, too. But Dan would have been better off hiring a general contractor. He cost himself valuable time. He subjected himself to a sort of personal torture—and certainly cost himself money, as the two or three months of unnecessary delays represented two or three months of business (and profit) that didn't happen.

Only you can make the decision as to whether you will benefit, as Madeline and Roger did, or not, as was the case with Danny.

An Alternative: The Manager's Contract If you feel inclined to be your own contractor but somehow you don't feel that it is quite within your abilities, you might consider hiring a construction manager.

As mentioned in Chapter 3, the construction manager can be an architect or a carpenter or even a small contractor. But instead of offering you a price for the whole job, the construction manager signs an agreement that specifies that he will be paid a fee that is a percentage of the total time and materials costs. If the basis for the fee is 10 percent and the time and materials costs come to $50,000, you will pay him $5,000 for his services as construction manager.

Getting a Construction Loan

In Chapter 5, we will discuss borrowing the money you need to pay for your construction. The same rules discussed there apply here, too, but as a GC you must keep in mind other concerns as well.

If you are going to act as your own GC and have never done so before, you should anticipate that some bankers you approach won't even consider your application. In fact, this first step in the process may be the single biggest hurdle you will face.

Bankers regard the novice GC as the kind of risk they don't need. Rookie contractors don't always finish the job, sometimes the job isn't done to code, and so on. Banks want to avoid seeing the paper they're holding from you turn into a liability rather than an asset.

There are, however, many bankers receptive to borrowers who can demonstrate to them the knowledge, good sense, and confidence needed to pull off the GC's job. But it is important that you get across to your banker that you can do the job and do it well.

One way to accomplish this is to deliver along with the rest of your paperwork a résumé of your construction experience. If you have none, then a general statement regarding your business experience may be useful. In particular, emphasize any demonstrable abilities or experience you have in buying services and materials or in managing people.

Be sure when you meet with the banker that you are well organized. You will need to have not only the financial paperwork in order but the construction documents as well, including the architectural plans, the estimates, and the construction schedule. The banker will want to come away from his meeting with you feeling not only that you can afford to do what you want to do but that you are clear on the plan, that you know specifically what it is going to cost, that you have arranged for properly trained and licensed people to do the work for you, and that you have the wherewithal to get it done.

Getting a loan involves more than a simple financial judgment on the part of your banker. He also wants to be confident that you are a responsible person. The last thing he wants is to put his approval on a loan only to see it go bad. Banks lose money on that kind of business, and as in every other business, the executives look to see who is making them money and who isn't.

Remember, in talking with your banker, that one argument in your repertoire is that by acting as your own GC you are saving money. Even allowing for the numerous ways of saving dollars an experienced general contractor can bring to a job, his markup will be far greater than those savings. If you're the GC, his 20 or 30 percent is a markup you don't have to spend—and money the bank doesn't have to loan.

Special Concerns

As a GC, you have a number of concerns you do not have as a client. Much advice contained in the following chapters will be applicable, too, but in the next few pages, we'll look at some others peculiar to those who assume the GC's role.

FINDING SUBS. This will be your job. And it is an important one, as these are the ladies and gentlemen who will actually build your house for you, and you want to make the right decisions in hiring them.

As with finding a GC, you must check each sub's references (customers, suppliers, banks, and others; see Chapter 3). Get several subs to estimate on the big jobs and at least two on the small ones (tiling the floor in one bathroom is a small job; installing the plumbing for an entire two-and-one-half-bathroom house with forced hot-water heat is a big one). Do your homework before you hire your people.

To find subs, check job sites you see in residential areas in your vicinity. Wander right in and ask for the plumbing contractor or the electrician. Often you will come away with a business card, at least a phone number, possibly an appointment, and maybe even an estimate if you have your plans in the car and he has an hour to kill.

Another good source of subs is supply houses. Ask at the suppliers that deal with the trades. You'll get a couple of names. Ask other contractors, too. Your carpenter may well have a plumber or two he trusts and an electrician he's worked with for years.

When it comes to dealing with subs, keep in mind that most of them bid on as many jobs as possible and often take on more than they can handle. The bad news is that you, as a one-time customer, are likely to be down toward the bottom of their priority list, well below the GCs who are going to be building many houses in the future and may be good customers for the sub's services. Get ready for the frustrations and scheduling hassles. The good news is that you are not alone: you have your subs to help you get the job done. They are there not only to get your house built but to help you do it. You may be surprised to find the pride that many individual operators in the construction business take in their work. Try to use that pride and spirit to your advantage.

The carpenter will be your primary sub, so ask him for help in finding an electrician, plumber, or mason. And don't worry too much about cronyism here. Most carpenters can be counted on to recommend people they like to work with but few will recommend subs who don't know their jobs. They know which are the guys who mess up the schedule and who do sloppy work and make trouble for everybody else.

You should also get each of your subs to do takeoffs for you. Get them to direct you to suppliers, even to do estimating themselves. You may want to compare the estimates they get with your own.

INSURANCE. When you act as your own GC, you'll need a builder's risk or fire policy. Check with your insurance agent. In most states, prices tend to vary only slightly from company to company because they are usually closely regulated. You will want to arrange for the insurance to be effective the moment the building materials arrive or the first worker sets foot on the site, whichever is earlier. If you have a construction loan, the bank may insist on the insurance being effective at the time you close on the loan. When the house is finished, you can simply arrange for a change in policy so that you will have a standard homeowner's policy.

TELEPHONE. In constructing a new house, put a phone on the job site. You can't be there every moment, and many questions and problems can be resolved simply by phone. Materials can be ordered, revised schedules established, and so on. The time to have the line put in is when the framing is underway.

By being your own contractor, you will eliminate a middleman from the process. That should save you a good deal of money, but it also gives you numerous responsibilities.

Most of those we have discussed above. You have to coordinate the activities of the subs. You have to set up schedules and pay bills and perform a number of other functions. But there's one other role you will have to assume as well.

As GC, you become the Harry Truman of the operation: you're the person with the "buck stops here" sign. The big and little decisions along the way are yours to make. There'll be professional help around to answer questions, but, finally, you pass the yeas and nays.

There's another key consideration. If you aren't satisfied at the end, you can't call your GC and tell him you won't make the last payment because this or that is not up to your standards.

This is perhaps the biggest single reason not to be your own GC. If you hire someone to do the job for you and then something goes wrong, it really isn't your problem. That's not absolutely true, of course, but in general a GC is paid to solve the problems and get the job done. You are paying for his experience, competence, good sense, and, more than anything else, for his willingness to assume final responsibility for the whole job.

If you assume that responsibility, keep in mind it represents some sleepless nights. And should major problems arise, you cannot call your lawyer and tell him, "Sue the damn GC, it's his fault." One of the laws of the land is that your wife can't testify against you in court; another is that you can't sue yourself.

Don't take this decision lightly. But if you opt for taking the job, you may be saving a good deal of money. And earning the satisfaction of having managed the whole thing yourself.

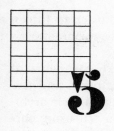

5

THE

ECONOMICS

*Loans and Contracts
and Paying the Bills*

A young, successful, career-oriented couple—let's call them Peter and Rachel—are expecting their first child. They've decided that the city apartment in which they've lived happily for the last few years isn't suitable for bringing up a baby.

They have definite ideas on what they need and want in their new house. Their tastes and concerns—an exercise area for him, a professional kitchen for her (Rachel's the cooking editor for a major women's magazine)—suggest that they need a specially designed house. So they go to an architect and present him with their answers to the questionnaire in Chapter 1. They also have established a budget of not more than $90,000.

A residential architect generally charges a fee of 15 percent of the total construction cost. That's a rule of thumb and must be taken in context. As we discussed in Chapter 2, a good architect may save you as much as he'll cost you, but when you look at the actual expenses of a typical job, you will see that from ten to fifteen cents out of every dollar goes into the architect's coffers.

After some give-and-take, the review of sketches and floor plans and catalogues and several meetings, Peter and Rachel and their architect settle on the plan. The architect, using current industry averages, has designed a house that suits their budget. To put it another way, although actual estimates have not been done by all the tradesmen needed to build the house, the plan calls for Peter and Rachel to spend the balance of their $90,000—that is, some $77,000—constructing the house.

Their next session is with a general contractor. He reviews their plans with them, studies the specifications, and then goes off to do his own calculations. Yet another negotiation ensues: the contractor says it will cost more like $85,000 to build the house as the architect specified.

The contractor, architect, and Peter and Rachel sit down and go through the plans. The architect and contractor present some suggestions for changes, and Peter and Rachel agree to downgrading the materials to be used on a couple of floors (two tile floors become linoleum, one wood floor wall-to-wall carpeting). They also agree to skip the carport for now ("We can live without it a year or two"). So the price comes down to $79,000.

As much as a third of a general contractor's estimate is his "gross margin." In the building trades, as in other businesses, the gross margin is margin allowed for profit and overhead. Thus, if Peter and Rachel's contractor calculated that the labor and materials cost of their home was $50,000, then he would add $25,000 for the gross margin. The first time around he came up with a little more, so they compromised in a couple of areas. But the result was that they got the contractor to agree to build their house for approximately what they wanted to pay; and he got his margin for profit and expenses. The contractor will use that gross margin to pay for office, insurance, travel, and other costs, as well as to give himself a profit.

Now we are ready to build, right? Not quite yet. This brings us to the heart of this chapter. Peter and Rachel, or any other typical customer planning to build or remodel, must now get themselves a loan and sign some contracts before proceeding with construction.

Professional Help

Before we talk about loans and contracts, however, it is important to get a little more help. According to the trade publication *Building Supply News*, two out of three home renovators are embarking on their virgin ventures into renovation. Most people who are having an entirely new home built for them are in the same situation. These people are going into business for themselves for just one project, and they can't afford to learn from their mistakes as they go.

In order to be assured that you are not headed for debtors' prison, it's a good idea to hire a lawyer and perhaps other assistance as well. These people won't be banging nails or even visiting the site, but your banker and attorney, in particular, are key players.

The Real Estate Attorney You may resent it, but the fact is that we live in a world where good legal counsel is essential to conducting business. While part of you may think of the home renovation or construction process in warm, emotional terms, it is also true that to buy the real estate and construction services and to sign a series of contracts is, by definition, to enter into a whole string of business deals.

You need a lawyer to look out for your interests. Your banker, the seller, the contractor, the architect, and the other players are unlikely to have the same concerns as you, so their counsels cannot be counted on to protect you.

Even if you hire a GC or use an architect to administer the whole process and never visit the site, you will need legal guidance for reviewing contracts and checking out zoning restrictions and numerous other matters. You may find that an experienced real estate attorney can help in ways you have never considered. He's already seen clients through most of the hassles you'll be facing, so his experience and advice can be invaluable, whether it is in negotiating the right contract at the start, working through a misunderstanding in the midst, or resolving a dispute long after completion.

Apart from the guidance you may get from your lawyer in dealing with miscellaneous questions or in brainstorming, you must have an attorney for your loan closing and land purchase (if any) and reviewing contracts.

If you have an established relationship with an attorney, be sure he is well versed in real estate law. Does he do a reasonable volume of real estate work? Even if he was your college roommate, check it out, because real estate law has its own complexities and can get just as arcane as any other area of the law. And mistakes can be very expensive. If you don't have a suitable lawyer, try calling a couple of nearby real estate agencies or mortgage departments at local banks and ask them for references. The local bar association is another potential source; ask for the chairman of the real estate committee.

The Banker If you are getting a loan of any kind, you need a banker. Later in this chapter we will discuss how to get a loan, but one consideration is the individual loan officer you deal with. As with all your professional advisers, your banker can be just another person across whose desk your paperwork travels from time to time. No law says you have to be best friends with your banker. On the other hand, you are an amateur in the business, and the more professional advice you can get, the better off you will be.

When it comes time to apply for a loan, do it in person. If possible, talk to the person who approves the loans or who screens them, and try to get a sense of how helpful he or she is inclined to be. You don't want someone who will talk your ear off about the petty details of this or that deal, but you do want someone who will listen to your questions and give you straight answers. Make sure you get all the attachments and instructions, and a clear understanding of the processes of approval and payment.

One good way to get a feel for the candor and accessibility of the banker is to ask for recommendations regarding contractors, architects, or lawyers. Many banks instruct their employees to avoid endorsing any individual not directly associated with the bank, so if you ask your question over the phone you will probably get an answer like "I'm sorry, it is our policy not to recommend lawyers to our customers." But if you are sitting across the desk from your banker, and you ask about Attorney Jones, you may get a more candid evaluation.

The key issue with your banker, however, is his or her willingness to help you deal with the red tape of the banking business. You should be able to get an immediate sense of whether the banker knows the application forms and the schedules and ordinary workings of the system at his bank. If he seems confused or unwilling to explain or facilitate your loan, find another banker.

Other Professionals Your architect may arrange for the services of a structural engineer. If your house is a Frank Lloyd Wright-like design with prestressed concrete cantilevering over a waterfall, the engineer's fee will be well invested. Make sure you establish with your architect what the engineering fee will be and who pays for it. You don't want a several-thousand-dollar surprise.

If you have an accountant who prepares your taxes, get his opinions and guidance early. Sit down with him and discuss your budget, loan arrangements, the cash flow of the project (you expect which bills in which month, which are this year and which next), and your income. He may be able to advise you on tax credits (some credits are available for the rehabilitation of older buildings) and other issues that could save you money.

Loans

Unless you have the cash on hand to pay for your project, you will need to borrow money. The first choice for most people is a bank loan.

A formula banks have traditionally used to establish how much money they can lend you is that your monthly carrying charges (mortgage payment, taxes, and, if applicable, cooperative or condominium fees) should be no more than 25 to 28 percent of your gross monthly income. For example, if your annual income is $60,000 a year and your monthly gross income, therefore, is $5,000, then according to this rule of thumb you can pay $1,200 to $1,400 a month in carrying charges. In today's market, with interest rates under 10 percent, that translates to a loan of roughly $140,000. (Another formula you may meet up with is an annual payment ceiling of two and one-half times your monthly income.)

However, in recent years the 25 to 28 percent range has not always been honored. Particularly when interests rates skyrocketed in the early eighties, it was necessary for some mortgagees to commit to 40 or 50 percent or an even higher percentage of income. This trend is most common in some urban areas where an automobile is not a necessity (meaning that no car payments are added to a mortgagee's total indebtedness). Few bankers have been heard to encourage such practices, however.

Find yourself a bank whose rates are low. Then find an individual within its offices who is helpful and cooperative. Then learn everything you can about that bank's likes and dislikes. Don't be surprised if you have to shop around a little before you find a bank you like and that will lend you the money you need.

Loans for New Construction

There are a variety of loans available, and with the advice of your lawyer and accountant you should find the one best suited to your needs.

CONVENTIONAL MORTGAGE. A conventional mortgage is a fixed-rate, self-amortizing mortgage. "Fixed rate" means that the interest rate established at the time the loan is granted remains the same throughout the term of the mortgage; "self-amortizing" means that at the conclusion of the mortgage's term the loan will have been paid off (i.e., "amortized").

ADJUSTABLE-RATE MORTGAGE. Conventional mortgages were the rule until the mid-seventies, but now a common option is the adjustable-rate mortgage (ARM). Sometimes called a "rollover" mortgage, an ARM will allow the bank to adjust the interest rate during the term of the mortgage. This kind of mortgage became popular because interest rates were varying almost daily.

In issuing an adjustable-rate mortgage, the lending institution will begin at an interest percentage below what they are offering for conventional mortgages. Then, on an agreed-upon annual date (usually the first day of the new year or one year after closing), the rate will be adjusted according to a formula based upon a financial market index (e.g., the prime rate).

Should you decide upon a variable-rate mortgage, be sure that there is a cap established (the rate can go no higher than a certain percentage) and that there is a limitation on the annual increases that can be made (no more than 2 percent per year is typical and reasonable).

BALLOON MORTGAGE. A balloon mortgage is one in which a large or "balloon" payment of the remaining principal is due at a specific date. Payments are made along the way, often of interest alone though in some cases token principal payments are made as well. Balloon mortgages are more common in real estate transactions for commercial or multi-family dwellings.

CONSTRUCTION LOAN. In the construction of an all-new house, few banks will issue a standard mortgage. Instead, you will want to apply for a combination construction loan and mortgage.

The construction loan is the bank's way of gradually paying out the construction money. They don't want to give you the chance to take all the money and let it run away with you. Rather, the bank is interested in assuring that their investment—namely, your house—is constructed according to the agreed-upon schedule and terms. So they will pay you in installments, with payments due at specific points in the construction process. When the house is completed, and the last of the construction loan payments have been made, the construction loan will be formally changed to a traditional mortgage loan identical to what you would apply for if you were buying a finished home instead of building one.

On a construction loan, you pay only interest on the money lent you. In fact, most contractors (who often finance their businesses through construction loans) regard the interest payments as a cost of construction rather than an out-of-pocket cost. That is, they anticipate making the monthly interest payments to the bank out of the money advanced by the bank.

A construction loan works like this: You apply for a loan for the estimated construction cost of your house. You must have a plan, a general contractor, the deed to the land, and the building permits and other paperwork all in order. You present the whole package to your banker.

If the bank approves the loan, they will present you with a disbursement schedule. This specifies that a certain percentage of the loan proceeds are due upon completion of the foundation, more upon the roof being finished, more at the time the windows are put in place, and so on. You build your house, and they pay you according to the schedule when they see that their requirements have been met.

Loans for Renovation Projects In the case of a renovation, there are a number of alternative sources of financing. One is a simple personal loan, another a second mortgage. If the renovation is relatively inexpensive, you may want to avoid the paperwork of loan applications and simply draw a cash advance from one or more of your credit cards, though the interest rates are generally rather high. Each of these methods of financing has advantages and disadvantages.

PERSONAL LOAN. A personal loan is a relatively simple transaction. You file an application with a lender, he checks your credit and indebtedness, and he approves or disapproves the application. The decision is made on the basis of your credit rating, income, and assets. It is an "unsecured" loan.

SECOND MORTGAGE. The second mortgage is a little more complicated, but is likely to be easier to get.

For practical purposes, a second mortgage is sort of a loan you give yourself. You go to the bank and file an application, but what the loan officer will look at most closely is the equity you have in your home.

Say, for example, you want to borrow $25,000 to improve your $100,000 home. The loan officer will determine what portion of your home you own. Let's say your original down payment was 25 percent of the purchase price and your pay-down on the principal since then equals another 25 percent. So you own half your house. That means you are a good candidate for that loan because most banks will loan up to 75 percent of the amount of equity (that is, the portion you have paid for in the existing house). And the bank will consider your house to be your collateral for the loan, making this a "secured" loan.

SELLER-FINANCED MORTGAGE. Seller-financed mortgages may be a practical alternative if you are buying an existing house with the expectation of renovating it.

Seller-financed mortgages can be conventional or fixed-rate or balloon mortgages. The difference is that the lending "institution" is the seller rather than a bank. Seller-financed mortgages became a practical alternative in the days of interest rates in the mid-teens, when sellers found that customers could ill afford the monthly

GETTING A LOAN

Banks are wary of losing the only asset they have, money. So they lend it only to people they think are to be trusted with it.

They establish your "trustworthiness" on numerous grounds, most obviously on the basis of your finances. The three key determining factors are your income, your credit record, and your assets and liabilities.

INCOME: The rule of thumb most often used for borrowing money is that your monthly loan payments should not exceed 25 to 28 percent of your gross monthly income. The bank will be concerned not only with your salaried income but with other sources of revenue, including stocks, bonds, trusts, and real estate.

In addition, if you are confident of a substantial increase in your income in the near future (for example, if your business has grown at a constant rate for each of the past five years), the projected future income is also an argument that can be used to convince a bank you are a good risk.

CREDIT RECORD: If you have previously applied for and been granted a mortgage and have subsequently paid some or all of it off, you are a better risk than someone who has never borrowed money in his life. Other indications that you are a good credit risk are a prompt payment history on previous personal loans, credit cards, and department store bills and the timely liquidation of other indebtedness.

ASSETS: In short, what do you own? A car? Another house? Other valuable belongings? The lender will regard it as a good sign if your down payment is coming from your savings. If you own your home and are renovating it, then your equity in the house is also a factor. Equity is defined as the present value of the house, less what you owe on it.

OTHER CONSIDERATIONS: If you own or control a business or have substantial financial resources of your own, you may already have a relationship with a particular bank. Try to use it to your best advantage. If you get the feeling you are not getting your due, go to another bank and make it clear that you are interested not only in a loan but perhaps in shifting other business their way as well. It might help.

payments bloated with interest expense. The seller would then offer short-term financing (five- and ten-year terms are common) at a reduced interest rate for some or all of the purchase price. The seller sells his house at or near his price, and the buyer can afford the monthly payments.

If you are buying a house with a renovation in mind, you may want to use some combination of bank and seller-financed mortgage, particularly if you are at or above what your bank sees as your lending ceiling. Consult your lawyer or accountant.

Another option for renovators is to renegotiate the current mortgage on your home. This makes especially good sense in cases where the existing mortgage is at an interest rate that is significantly higher than current prevailing rates. You may, in fact, be able to negotiate a new mortgage at a lower rate, pay the interest points at the closing for the new mortgage, get a lump sum of cash for your improvements, and end up with the same monthly payment.

Contracts

Christine and Charles bought a nineteenth-century brownstone on a picturesque street in Baltimore. They both needed offices at home (he's a professor, she's a psychologist), so the frontage on the street was perfect. They looked forward to having a backyard garden, room for her son by a previous marriage, plenty of space for entertaining, and two apartments above to pay some of the bills.

That's the good news. The other side of the story is that they got the building at an affordable price because it was a disaster area. The last owner had rented it to people who knew he didn't care, so they didn't either. Just cleaning the place out was a major job for Charles and Christine, not to mention that the plumbing and wiring had to be redone.

Charles had done a fair amount of construction work himself in years past, what with remodeling a kitchen here and reshingling a new roof there. But this was the first major renovation project for both of them.

Almost immediately they found a contractor they liked. He was new to the area, but was knowledgeable about the period of their building and seemed to understand intuitively the feeling they wanted their new home to have. And his estimate was within their budget.

So they came to an agreement with him. It was verbal, but they liked him. They gave him some money to get going and he did. Going where, they never have found out. They haven't seen him—or their money—ever since.

The first fact about contracts is that you need them. It's that simple. The paper trail continues, from your preliminary questionnaire and drawings, through to actual estimates and, eventually, to your canceled checks and the certificate of occupancy.

Contracts should be in writing. Always. In most states, it's not a binding contract if it's not in writing, and even if it is binding, when it comes to arguments, whose recollection is right? Get it on paper. As Samuel Goldwyn once said: "An oral agreement isn't worth the paper it's written on."

It's obvious, of course, that the name "contractor" comes from the word "contract." You meet with the contractor, describe the job to him, he gives you a price, and you agree upon the other terms of the agreement. A contract is made (orally at first, then in writing) that obligates the contractee to pay the contractor for the agreed-upon work.

A basic fee-plus arrangement makes sense for your architect, but you are better off not paying your contractor(s) on a fee-plus basis. Instead, you pay them a fixed price.

Your contracts should be signed by both parties and should bind both sides to the terms and conditions spelled out in the agreement. Generally that means the contractor will be obliged to provide certain materials and to perform certain services for you; in turn, you will be required to pay for those goods and that labor.

A contract should, however, specify, in as much detail as possible, the work to be done. The materials to be used should be listed, not only the quantity but also brand names and model numbers and specifications and dimensions and weight and quality and color and other details. A schedule for the work should be specified, as well as the prices and the terms of payment.

Contracts vary. The one you sign with the bank for a loan will probably be the most elaborate. And you don't have much say in that, as it is likely to be a standard contract that, no matter how tough a negotiator your lawyer is, he won't get changed very much.

Your bank may require that you have ready-to-sign contractual agreements with your contractor(s) in hand (or at least detailed estimates) before they give you the money to pay the bills.

Often contracts begin life as estimates. If you are adding a deck off your kitchen, the contractor may arrive at your home one evening, discuss with you the job to be done, inspect the site, and then retire to his clipboard. He is likely to use a standard estimate contract form, and may well, before your very eyes, write down your name, address, a description of the work to be done and the materials to be used, and then sign the sheet and hand it to you for your consideration. If you agree, he may ask you to sign right then and there and also to advance a portion of the price. He may promise to begin work in the morning.

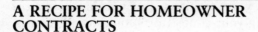

A RECIPE FOR HOMEOWNER CONTRACTS

All contracts you sign should begin with the parties to the agreement. Yours and the contractor's names and addresses should be stated up front, along with the date the agreement was drawn and a statement about the work to be done. This should cover each of the stages in the process and should describe the job in as much detail as possible. If the job requires cutting into the existing structure (to install electrical or plumbing lines, for example), the contract should specify whose responsibility it is to patch and repaint.

The rest of the ingredients are these:

THE SITE: The area and the limits of the job should be specified (the shingles on the house, not on the attached garage). Trash removal should also be specified. The term "broom clean" may be useful; insert the statement: "The job shall not be deemed completed until the premises are broom clean and all trash and unused materials removed."

THE MATERIALS: Detail is important throughout the estimate, but never more so than here. The specifications, as the materials list is commonly called, should include the brand names, dimensions, style, color, weight, and other identifying characteristics of all the materials to be used.

THE WARRANTY: What is the warranty? If there is one for all of the work or even a part of it, it should be spelled out here. Oral representations are more often forgotten than remembered.

THE LIABILITY: A copy of the contractor's insurance certificate should be attached to the agreement and mentioned here, along with words to the effect that the contractor will not hold the homeowner

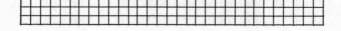

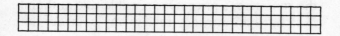

responsible in the event of any personal injury or property damage.

THE SCHEDULE: When does the work begin and when is it to be finished? Put in specific dates.

THE COST: The total cost and the schedule of payments belong here. We will talk about payment schedules shortly, but as a rule you only want to pay for work completed and paying less now and more later gives you maximum leverage.

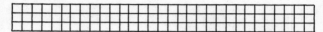

Use your own judgment: it may make sense to hire him, you may want it done right away, you may trust this fellow, especially if you have worked with him before. At the same time, however, be advised that in general you are better off if you take your time and give the decision proper consideration. Just ask Charles and Christine.

Some questions you should know the answer to are:

Does this contractor do quality work? The only way to know is to check out some of his previous jobs/references.

Is this a fair price? If you have two or more comparable estimates you can make a good judgment here, but if his is your only one, how can you be sure? Getting at least three is a good practice.

Is this piece of paper fair to you? This book can provide you with some guidance here, as in the following pages we will discuss payment schedules and other considerations, but especially if the document is long and packed with tiny print, get your lawyer to have a look. (If the cost of the work being contracted for is small, you may not want to spend the time and money in getting your lawyer to review it. It may not make sense if the attorney's fees will be greater than the contractor's price. One sensible rule of thumb is to have an attorney review any contract that will cost you more than what you make in two weeks.)

Do you understand every word? In many states, the law requires that contracts be written in plain language, but whatever the case in your area, be sure you understand what you are signing. Don't be fooled by complicated locutions like "heretofore" and "notwithstanding" into agreeing to something you don't mean.

Does the contract incorporate every piece of paper that has gone between the two signers of the contract? That includes the plans

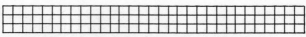

THE TWENTY-FOUR-HOUR RULE

Whether it's a big decision or a small one, don't get strong-armed. We've all heard stories about the piece of real estate that had to be bought immediately or it would be gone, and some of them are true. But don't believe it if someone tells you that the job he is going to do for you has a today-only price tag on it. It's often just part of the hard sell.

Instead of getting yourself talked into a deal that you are not sure is right for you, tell the person trying to sell you his goods or services that you made your grandfather a deathbed promise that you'd never make up your mind about a significant purchase until you had considered it overnight. Chances are the seller will wait the extra day.

Use the time to consider the situation. Consult with your advisers, get another estimate if you need one. Get comfortable with the deal. Then, twenty-four hours later, call the seller with your decision, whether you are buying or not. You owe him that courtesy, just as he owes it to you to give you the opportunity to make up your mind.

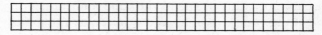

and the specifications you gave the contractor and the estimate and any changes he gave you in return. Remember, only written representations will stand the test of most courts.

Standard form contracts are available from the American Institute of Architects (check your phone book for the local chapter or write to the Institute at 1735 New York Avenue, N.W., Washington, D.C. 20006).

Contract Terms

PAYMENT TERMS. In a recent Hollywood release called *The Money Pit,* co-stars Tom Hanks and Shelley Long hire contractors to fix their disaster area of a house. The first thing they do is write a check for $5,000, without blinking an eye.

While the contractor did eventually get the job done, the moral of the story is you should never pay substantial dollars in advance. The principle to follow is that money should change hands on the basis of completed work, not talk or paperwork.

Some contractors may ask for substantial payments up front. In general, however, there is no reason to pay in advance. The building trades traditionally operate on a work-first, pay-later basis. Some contractors will insist upon some advance payment, but before you advance anybody money, be sure you have checked his references thoroughly, and even then, never, ever advance more than 10 or 15 percent of the total cost. If the contractor is insistent on more, find another contractor.

Not that you can pay months or years later. You will negotiate a payment schedule fair to both parties. The simplest guidelines for payment schedules are that no more than 10 to 15 percent should be paid up front; at least 15 to 20 percent should be withheld until completion; and all payments in between should be made only on completion of specific portions of the job.

The payment of bills is your best single method of controlling quality. You pay when the work is done properly and not before.

THE LUMP-SUM CONTRACT. For a straightforward job without lots of frills (the use of off-the-shelf materials, for example, to execute a straightforward design), the lump-sum contract is often best, for both you and the contractor. In this arrangement, your contractor will look at your plans, the specs, and, if the job involves an existing building, he will look at the job site, too. Then he'll give you a price. If no changes are made after his estimate is submitted, he will be obligated to hold to that price.

The lump-sum contract is simple and establishes before construction begins what the cost will be. However, if you elect to go with this method, make sure you get three or more estimates. When you get a lump-sum estimate, you won't see a breakdown of materials and labor costs, so it is impossible to tell from the estimate whether the contractor's markup for profit and overhead is 10 percent or 100 percent. If you have several estimates, you have a basis for comparison.

COST-PLUS OR TIME AND MATERIALS. In this method of payment, you and your contractor will agree on a percentage—say, 10 to 20 percent—for his fee. He will then charge his actual costs for time and materials plus the percentage. A job with labor and materials costs of, say, $50,000, with an agreed-upon fee of 20 percent for the contractor, would then cost you $60,000.

The most obvious disadvantage of such cost-plus contracts is that the more the contractor spends, the more he makes. There is no incentive for him to keep costs low, as there is when a price is established up front that he knows he has to live with. On the other hand, when it comes to jobs involving retrofitting an older house or where there are numerous unknowns (your final decisions on materials haven't been made yet, for example), few contractors will give you a lump-sum price. They can't estimate on what they don't know.

Make sure you check your contractor's references doubly carefully if you decide upon a time-and-materials arrangement.

UPSET PRICE. One way of establishing an upper limit while retaining the flexibility of a cost-plus arrangement is to get the contractor to agree to do the work on what is known as an "upset price" basis. Here, you both agree to a top price before he begins the job. Then he proceeds on a cost-plus basis.

When the job is finished, if the price is less than the upset price in the contract, you pay less; if it is more, it's his problem, and you pay no more than the upset price. However, the simpler, fixed-price arrangement is best if you can get the contractor to agree.

HOURLY RATE. Some smaller contractors may ask to work for hourly wages rather than for a fixed fee. They may say that in the end it will probably be cheaper for you.

Well, that's possible, if rather unlikely. It is recommended that you insist upon establishing a price up front. That way you won't have any surprises down the road. In addition, you avoid having employees and the extra paperwork required.

RETAINAGE. Another contractual strategy for controlling the job is retainage. When a payment is due, you pay 90 percent of the sum payable and retain the other 10 percent. The idea is to enhance your clout with your contractors. The unpaid percentage is due upon substantial completion of the job, and will be specified in the contract. Retainage, however, is to be negotiated along with the other parts of the deal, not unilaterally practiced when bill-paying time comes. Your contractors have to budget their revenues, too. Retainage can be used with the lump-sum, upset-price, or other contractual arrangements.

DRAW. Some contractors, especially smaller subs with limited working capital, will ask for a "draw" arrangement. Though every draw is a little different, the basic idea is to negotiate a fair balance of payment and work done. For example, a drywall contractor might ask to be paid each week for work completed. You might suggest that a value be assigned to each of the rooms being done. The large living room might be 50 percent of the whole, the two other, smaller rooms 25 percent apiece. He might say that actually hanging the gypsum board is approximately half the job, while the application of the tape and joint compound constitutes the balance. So he might, for example, ask to be paid a quarter of the whole contract price at the end of the first week if he finishes hanging the gypsum board in the living room. And so on.

One reputable restoration contractor I know of in New Jersey estimates what the whole job will cost, divides by the number of weeks required for completion, and then asks to get that sum at the end of each week.

Such arrangements as these are eminently fair to both parties, so long as work progresses as scheduled. Make sure, however, in the case of jobs that require inspections by the building department that the bulk of the money is paid only after the inspections have been made. And as we discussed in Chapter 3, make sure it is the contractor's responsibility to handle the inspections. In a typical case, a plumber might ask to be paid 50 or 60 percent of the total price when the "rough-in" is completed. That's fair enough, as long as the work has passed inspection. You will have to use your instincts and good sense as to what portion of a given job is done (if you have an architect guiding you, he should make these decisions), but if it's a quarter complete, don't pay a third.

An excellent clause to negotiate into a contract is one that states that should the completion of the job be delayed for an unreasonable period of time, then you may use the unpaid balance of the contract to hire someone else to finish the job. The clause must specify what is the expected schedule (thereby defining what is "reasonable"), and may also require notification (i.e., that you must advise the contractor that he has a few days or a week to get his act together or else). But it does provide you with an option in the event you find yourself wedded to an untrustworthy contractor.

LIQUIDATED DAMAGES CLAUSES. For practical purposes, liquidated damages clauses are penalty clauses (in fact, by law in some jurisdictions, these clauses are not enforceable, as they are held to be penalties).

Liquidated damages clauses do make their way into construction contracts from time to time, but, as a general rule, they create as many problems as they solve. If a contractor is going to be late and there is a penalty clause in his contract, you can bet he is going to blame the delays on someone else. And who is to say he's wrong?

More often than not, penalty clauses succeed only in creating arguments. Putting a specific schedule in the contract is important and probably as valuable as a penalty clause.

CHANGE ORDERS. Change orders are not part of the original contract, but are formal amendments to that agreement. They are issued when something about the job changes: materials are switched, the design is amended, or some unanticipated complication appears.

Change orders don't have to be complicated, but if the job changes, then the change orders must be done. They are a key part of the paper trail you are creating in order to control your project.

Bookkeeping

THE ESTIMATE SHEET. Before you sign on any contractors, collect all your estimates and create one sheet of paper that neatly aligns all your expenses in one column and your revenues (e.g., loan proceeds) in another; leave columns three and four blank. The estimate sheet doesn't have to be fancy, but it should be complete and accurate. Check the totals at least twice. You might also have one of your professional advisers review it with you, especially if you do not routinely prepare budgets.

If the bottom line tells you that you can afford to proceed, do so. But don't abandon the estimate sheet. As you sign contracts and pay bills, enter the real costs in the third and fourth columns. Keeping a continuous check on your expenditures is crucial to monitoring progress. That way you will be the first to know when your budget is in trouble, and you can take steps to solve the problem. And if one or another item comes in under budget, don't get so excited that you go out and spend the money. Construction jobs always have ups and downs (building materials are commodities traded daily, so their prices change from day to day), so savor the good news, but expect some other expense to come along and swallow the surplus.

CHECKING ACCOUNT. Unless your project is very small and involves only a handful of checks to contractors and suppliers, it's a good idea to open a separate checking account for the duration of your construction project. All loan proceeds should be deposited directly into it. All expenses should be paid by check out of it. Keep your day-to-day finances separate from the new account.

THE LOGBOOK. You may find it useful later in settling disputes, large and small, if you keep a daily log as things proceed. Take pictures of the job, too, as it progresses. That way, you can jog your memory—and other people's—when there are questions of who said or did what to whom and when.

The Last Word: How to Make "Not Enough" Enough
The second most significant problem encountered in the construction business (after unscrupulous operators) is the client who knows clearly what he wants but is unwilling—or unable—to spend what his dream will realistically cost.

What do you do if the estimates you receive from the contractors add up to a sum much greater than you had budgeted? Sit down with your architect, especially if he took part in the creation of that original budget. Review the estimates with him and see where the bulges are.

It's a good idea to have separate sessions with both the architect and the GC, if you have them, and ask them for strategies for cost reduction. The first approach should be to work within the design you have. What materials can be changed? Is there some portion of the job that can be postponed a year or two (leave one room as raw space until that baby you're thinking about having is more than simply a thought)?

If you still have budget troubles, is there a logical portion of the design that can be lopped off? The second bay in the garage? Do you need that extra deck off the second bedroom? When it comes to design changes, your architect is absolutely essential.

If you get contradictory advice from the contractor and the architect, you decide what is important, then have a meeting with both of them. Let them make their cases to one another, as well as you, and then make the decision. It's your nickel, so be satisfied.

A warning: Don't be penny-wise and pound-foolish. Take care not to eliminate something crucial just to trim the budget. Make a priority list of potential cuts from the project, and do your cutting from the bottom up. And try to take a big-picture approach. Don't end up compromising the whole just to save the hot tub. Consider adding later what you can't afford now.

6

THE CONSTRUCTION

The Dream Takes Shape

"Gentlemen, start your engines."

It's a simple imperative statement, but to the drivers and crowd alike at the Indianapolis 500, the announcement means an instant rush of adrenaline. The race is about to begin.

When the work begins on your construction project, such fanfare is unlikely and certainly the crowd will be smaller. But the excitement will still be there.

Officially, the construction phase of your project starts the moment you hire the builder to do the work. With the finished plans and a signed contract in hand, your direction is clear. The men (and perhaps women) will arrive in their vans or pickups, carrying their tools. Depending on the job, you'll see anywhere from one or two workers to dozens of them; the materials may fit neatly into the trunk of a single car, or require repeated visits from flatbed trucks.

Change Orders Even before we begin, we're talking about changes? Well, yes, but for good reason.

Before the work gets underway, try to make the plans and specifications as absolutely, definitely final as you can. Because your changes of mind later are going to cost you.

As discussed in the last chapter, change orders are the pieces of paper that you and the contractor should sign when something is changed from the original specs in his estimate. The change order will specify the changes (including the additional material and labor) and what the cost will be.

Going to the dentist is to be dreaded, weddings are fun, funerals are sad occasions, and change orders are expensive. No matter how fair your contractors are, it's another kind of tradition that every change order costs more than you think it will.

One reason the cost generally goes up is that a contractor makes money by plying his trade, not by doing paperwork. He had to do an estimate to get your job, but now that he has a contract with you there is no incentive to underbid anybody. So make up your mind early on what you want, and expect high costs for changes later.

You should follow two basic rules with change orders. First, if you are using an architect, have him negotiate them (he may know an inexpensive solution and, in any case, he probably knows more about buying construction services than you do). Second, get the change order in writing.

In the balance of this chapter, we will outline the steps followed by your builders in constructing your project. There are two major subsections. If you are building an entirely new space, then the portion of this chapter called "The Construction Process" is for you. On the other hand, if your job involves only interior remodeling within an existing house, you may want to skip to "The Remodeling Process" (see page 147). That way, you won't be confronted with the steps that don't apply to you, such as the new foundation and roofing work.

Regardless of which kind of job you are doing, don't be surprised if some of the steps in your project vary from those described here. Everyone has his own way of doing things. Some general contractors put the wood floors down before the drywall goes up, whereas others think that is hilariously wrongheaded. Your GC knows what works best for him.

The Construction Process

The Excavation and the Foundation The surveyor goes to work first. Armed with a transit, an instrument that establishes elevations and levels and points, he will mark off the location of the house, garage, or addition, regardless of topographical variations. He will need your plot plan, which should have any setbacks and other restrictions marked on it. He will leave stakes and, in some cases, connecting strings, to indicate where the excavation should be done. The stakes are usually some distance outside the actual location of the foundation or cellar hole.

One small caution: Don't faint dead away if the staked-out space looks awfully small. Even big houses seem minute when reduced to two dimensions and viewed under the canopy of the sky. If it makes you feel better, put your tape measure to the stakes, but you'll probably only succeed in insulting your surveyor and making yourself feel a little silly.

It's a good idea to be on site during the surveyor's visit. He will probably require only a couple of hours to do his job, so it won't cut a big hole in your schedule. And you can be sure he's putting the house where you want it. It isn't critical that you be there during the excavation and foundation work, but someone—either you or your architect—must be sure to establish that the foundation is located where it should be and fits the specifications.

At this point, the men in their magnificent earthmoving machines arrive. The bulldozers and the rest move like turtles, but then they weren't bred for speed. They'll remove gargantuan quantities of soil, as well as tree stumps and miscellaneous boulders (any giant ones may require blasting or drilling). They will leave you with a foundation hole dug to a depth of at least six inches below the frost line.

The frost line is the depth to which the frost penetrates the earth. The base or "footing" of the foundation must be beneath the frost line to prevent the frost from heaving portions of your foundation and causing your house to settle unevenly. (The deeper frost lines in northern areas are one reason why full basements are more common there.) If there are connections to be made to municipal sewage and water lines, the trenches for those hookups will also be dug at this point.

The potential problems during the excavation process are too many rocks, too much water (an underground stream or spring may require special drainage), or soil that isn't capable of holding the weight of your house. In parts of the country where soil problems are common, your realtor, lawyer, or bank will probably have suggested that you test it in advance.

Now that you have a hole in the ground, the foundation can be built. The first step is the footing, usually a base of cement wider than the wall to be constructed on it which will distribute the weight over a larger area to prevent settling. The wall itself comes next (after the concrete sets, which takes an average of three to five days). The wall may be of cement block or of concrete poured into a constructed wooden form that is removed after the concrete has set. Stone foundations are almost unheard of these days, though for aesthetic reasons some concrete foundations are built with a small shelf set into the portion of the foundation that will be above grade (i.e., not buried) onto which a veneer of brick or stone can laid to hide the less attractive concrete.

When the walls are finished, perforated

piping (called drain tiles) is laid outside the wall at its base. These will be pitched to allow the water that enters them to drain off and away from the foundation.

The earthmoving equipment will then return and backfill around the cellar hole. The soil on the surface must be graded in such a way that rainwater will naturally flow away from the house rather than into its foundation. (This work is done by a bulldozer or other earthmoving machinery, and is called cutting and filling, as the blade of the bulldozer serves to cut off the tops of the high spots and fill in the low ones.) If you are planning on any landscaping work, now is the time to give the yard at least an approximate shape, while the heavy equipment is there filling in around the cellar hole.

Rough Construction The carpenters arrive once the foundation is complete. They construct the wooden framing for the walls and floors and ceilings and roof of the house. (Even if the exterior is brick, the interior framing is going to be of wood. Commercial construction and an occasional residential job will employ only brick, steel, concrete, and materials specified for fireproof construction, but chances are your house will be of traditional wood-frame construction.)

While the framing work is going on, any conversation you listen in on will probably involve some new words. A stud is a vertical wall member; a joist is a horizontal floor support; a post is usually a larger corner stud; and a beam is a large horizontal member. The roof is supported by rafters.

On the outside of the stud walls the carpenters will apply plywood or some other sheet material. It's called sheathing when it's on the wall, but when the same or similar material is on the floor it's called the subfloor. On the exterior of the sheathing, a layer of tar-impregnated paper or some other water-repellent substance (often called "building paper") will be attached.

Framing does not require the kind of

precise (and time-consuming) attention to detail that finish work does, so inspecting the work site after a week's or even a day's labor can be very satisfying. Rooms seem to emerge almost overnight, and you can suddenly get a sense of how the new spaces will appear and relate to one another.

During the framing process, you and/or your architect should spend some time measuring and inspecting carefully to be sure that the partitions as constructed coincide with the plans. It's probably a good idea to put your tape measure to use after hours. There is no need to insult the carpenters, although they know as well as you do that, no matter how experienced they are, they're still capable of making a mistake.

Check window and door locations and sizes. If you find any discrepancies at all, discuss them first with whoever is supervising the construction. If it's your architect, let him have the hard conversation with the builder. But do it sooner rather than later. Every nail that gets put in makes it harder to undo what's been done.

If to your horror you discover that something just isn't working (that little study you put in is simply too small, for example), now is the time to make the change. It will probably cost you money, but you must make the judgment as to whether you want to live with it for years or pay the price now.

If you're a believer in tradition or are superstitious, you may want to perform an ancient ritual at the time the ridgepole is raised. (The ridgepole is the uppermost horizontal piece of lumber to which the rafters attach at the peak of the roof.) Early colonists brought with them a tradition of placing an evergreen bough—a symbol of permanence—at the roof's highest point. Don't clamber up there yourself, however. Ask a laborer to do it for you.

The Mechanical Systems Rough-Ins When the framing is complete, the electricians and plumbers and HVAC subs will arrive to begin their work. The electricians will be drilling holes through studs and joists to pull their wires through, the plumbers installing their pipes, the heating, ventilation, and air-conditioning contractors their ducts and/or piping. The phone men and, if you require one, the alarm installers, too, do their preliminary work now. If you are planning on a built-in sound system or intercom, this is the time for the rough wiring for those systems as well. If the foundation of your new structure is simply a slab, much of the plumbing rough-ins would have been completed before the slab was poured, along with any portions of the mechanical systems that are there (in some cases steam or electric lines).

The local building inspector will probably have visited during the foundation work, but he's guaranteed to come now. In fact, different inspectors may arrive to look at plumbing, electrical, and other work. Again, this should not be your problem. Your subs should be responsible for arranging for—and passing—the inspections.

The electrical and plumbing work probably won't look very familiar to you at this stage. The pipes won't be attached to fixtures, but will end at the planes of the wall and floor. The electrical work will consist of stretching wires from one end of the house to the other, all of which return to the main panel, which will resemble Medusa's head, only the hairdo is of wires rather than snakes.

Most of the mechanical work done at this stage will be hidden behind walls and ceilings. It is relatively simple to run a pipe or wire through the bare bones of a wall (the studs), but much more difficult later when the skin of gypsum board or other material has been applied.

Once the mechanical rough-ins are complete, thick blankets or "batts" of fiberglass insulation will be stapled between the studs on exterior walls. If you are around when this process is being done, wear a mask—or at least a handkerchief—over your mouth and nose, as the particles of fiberglass are, literally, tiny shards of glass that can be harmful to your lungs. And wear long sleeves, too.

A last step before the finished wall surface is applied is the installation of a vapor barrier. This important step is simple. It requires only that a thick layer of plastic be applied on the inside of all exterior walls.

The vapor barrier serves two purposes that are especially important in colder climes. One is to prevent condensation from building up in the walls. The vapor barrier, as its name suggests, prevents moisture in the air of the home from traveling outward through the walls to where it is colder and condensation might occur. Moisture in the walls could reduce the effectiveness of the insulation, but more important, it could also lead to decay of the wood structure. The other value of the vapor barrier is to prevent the infiltration of cold air from the outside. It is airtight and will help keep air from leaking through any chinks in the walls.

Roofing and Siding Roofing and siding materials are crucial to the life of the house. They protect the interior and its inhabitants, in particular from the principal enemy of any house, water.

You and your architect/designer, along with your pocketbook, will have decided what the materials will be. If your construction project is a remodeling or an addition to an existing house, then presumably you will have chosen the same material as what is already there or material that is compatible with it.

The roof will go on first. The siding follows, and while it is being installed, interior work can be completed in a dry environment. If your project has a fireplace or chimney scheduled, it should be completed before the shingling is done.

A crucial part of all exterior work involves "flashing." Flashing is metal (aluminum or copper) or plastic film. It is applied in strips to areas where dissimilar materials adjoin: where the masonry chimney meets the asphalt shingles, where the siding abuts the window frames, and so on. Good flashing work is critical to keeping a structure watertight, as the most likely place for leakage to occur is where different materials meet.

Walls and Ceilings The completed rough frame of the structure allows you to get a physical and visual sense of the new or renovated space. You may have to squint a little, but the shape of the space is there. However, it is only after the walls and ceilings are installed that you will get a clear sense of the final feel and dimension of the rooms.

You and your architect should have decided long before this moment what material is to be used for wall and ceiling surfaces, but the common options these days are gypsum board (also called drywall and Sheetrock) and wood paneling.

The gypsum board comes in sheets, four feet wide and of various lengths depending upon the dimensions of the walls to be covered. The sheets are applied to the walls with specially designed nails or screws whose heads are recessed just beneath the surface of the gypsum board. After all the sheets are in place, a number of layers of plaster-like paste called joint compound are applied. The joint compound covers the nail or screw holes and, along with strips of tape, the joints between the sheets. Gypsum board ceilings are done in the same way. Most drywall is a dull gray color, but waterproof drywall, which is often required (and always a good idea) in kitchens and baths, is usually a bluish-green color.

In the case of paneling, prefabricated, veneered sheets are available, as are precut widths of solid boards. With the veneered sheets, the finish has already been applied: it saves time and money, but generally looks like it did, too. You and your architect will have to resolve what gives you the look you want at a price you can afford.

The Finish Work Now comes the hardest part. You look around you at the new walls and ceilings. You consider how much work has gone in already and how much is really finished. And it feels like you're in the bottom of the ninth and are only an out or two away from celebrating victory.

Not so fast, as the saying goes. Finish work often seems to take a disproportionately long time. But good finish work can make your new house or space just right; on the other hand, poor finish work can render the whole job suddenly unsuccessful.

This is not to say you should allow the carpenters and other tradesmen to come and go and finish at a snail's pace while they are working on other people's jobs. It is to say that even though you feel like the finish line is looming up just ahead, you still have to pace yourself.

The finish work falls into two basic categories, the mechanical installations and the surface finishes.

MECHANICAL INSTALLATIONS. The plumbers put in your toilet and sink at this stage (it's called "trimming out" or "setting the fixtures"). The electricians will install your dining-room chandelier and your electric range. The plugs and light switches get tied in now, and the power comes on, too. The mechanical work must be meticulously coordinated with the surface finish work: the toilet goes on top of the tile floor, so the tile man must do his bit before the plumber can do his.

SURFACE FINISHES. Surface work includes everything from putting down the tile, wood, or carpeting on the floors to hanging the doors and applying the casings around the windows and doors, and moldings at the baseboard and ceiling. Kitchens get their cabinets. Doorknobs and window latches get attached. Switch and plug covers are applied. Painting gets done, too, along with a thousand other things.

This is a time when your inspections are most important. You should be available to the workers, but not in their way. Often there are many questions that come up at the last minute, and if they know you are there to answer their questions—or will be at a certain time—you're more likely to get what you want.

On the other hand, if in your visits to the work site you notice that the moldings don't match at one point or that a door doesn't close, don't take it upon yourself to bring up every nit and pick with the nearest workman, or even with his boss. Make a list.

There's a term in the building trades for this list of corrections. It's called a "punch list." The punch list isn't a daily gift for your architect or contractor. Give it to him once a week, perhaps even on the same day each week. Keep a copy for yourself, too, and follow up before you give him the next one to make sure what you asked for got done. If it didn't, find out why.

The punch list is a key part of getting the job completed.

The Last Details

THE SITE. After your contractor has completed his job, he should clean up his mess. There shouldn't be chunks of wood left embedded in the soil (they're lures for termites). Your driveway shouldn't be adorned with a pile of nails. His tools and equipment and materials should disappear along with him and his workmen.

If your contract called for landscaping, grading, or plantings, have they been completed to specification? How about walks and patios and driveways?

(If your project is new construction rather than remodeling, skip to page 152.)

The Remodeling Process

Rough Construction You're lucky, you remodelers, you don't have to worry about a big hole in your yard. You also don't have to worry about the framing of the building or the roofing. (That is, unless you're adding a dormer or otherwise amending the existing roof, in which case you should read the "Roofing and Siding" section, above.)

On the other hand, if you live in the house, you're not so lucky, especially if you are planning to live there while the job is being done. The builders will have to work around you and the lives being led by your family members, and you must do the same for the workers.

At best, this is a hassle. Think about it this way: Remember that blue suit that always seems to have lint on it? Well, how will you feel if your whole life has lint on it? The lint will actually be sawdust and gypsum dust, but take my word for it, it'll be everywhere. Therefore, if there is any way to avoid living at the job site, do it. If there simply isn't, then make sure you and your contractor have a special planning session in which he briefs you on the steps in the process and what he expects you to do—and not to do—at points along the way.

The carpenters are most likely to be the first to arrive to get your interior remodeling underway, and their first task is likely to be demolition. Those kitchen cabinets you have always hated will be removed or the cracked tiles in the old bath will have to be sledgehammered down and out. The demolition is the first of the messy, dusty work.

Once the old is gone, the new will be put in its place. The carpenters will construct the wooden framing for the walls and, if any, for the new floors and ceilings. Some apartments require brick, steel, concrete, and materials specified for fireproof construction, but chances are your home is of traditional wood-frame construction, so you won't require tradesmen other than carpenters for the rough construction.

The conversations you listen in on while the framing work is going on will probably involve some words that are new to you. A stud is a vertical wall member; a joist is a horizontal floor support; a post is usually a larger corner stud; and a beam is a large horizontal member. Consult the Glossary (page 169) if you are bashful about asking your contractor to define new words for you.

Framing doesn't demand the kind of precise (and time-consuming) attention to detail that finish work does, so inspecting the work site after the workers have been there only a day or two can be very satisfying. New spaces seem to emerge almost overnight, and you can suddenly get a sense of how the rooms will appear and relate to one another.

While the carpenters are framing, you and/or your architect should spend some time measuring and inspecting carefully to be sure that the partitions as constructed coincide with the plans. It's probably a good idea to put your tape measure to use after hours. There is no need to insult the carpenters, although they know as well as you do that, no matter how experienced they are, they're still capable of making a mistake.

Check door locations and sizes. If you find any discrepancies from the plans or even the space you've been seeing in your imagination, discuss them first with whoever is supervising the construction. If your architect is inspecting for you, let him have the hard conversation with the contractor-carpenter. But do it sooner rather than later. Every nail that gets put in makes it harder to undo what's been done.

If to your horror you discover that something just isn't working (the little foyer is simply too little, for example) now is the time to make the change. It will probably cost you money, but you must make the judgment as to whether you want to live with it for years or pay the price now.

The Mechanical Systems Rough-Ins When the framing is complete, the electricians and plumbers and HVAC subs will arrive to begin their work. The electricians will be drilling holes through studs and joists to pull their wires through, the plumbers doing the same for their pipes, the heating, ventilation, and air-conditioning contractors for their ducts and/or piping. The phone men and, if you require one, the alarm installers, too, do their preliminary work now. If you are planning on a built-in sound system or intercom, this is the time to put in the rough wiring for those systems.

The local building inspector will also arrive about this time. In fact, different inspectors may arrive to look at plumbing, electrical, and other work. This should not be your problem, as your subs should be responsible for arranging for the inspections—and passing them.

The electrical and plumbing work probably won't look very familiar to you at this stage. The pipes won't be attached to fixtures, but will end at the planes of the wall and floor. The electrical work will consist of stretching wires from the new area back to your main panel.

Most of the mechanical work done at this stage will eventually disappear behind walls and ceilings. It is relatively simple to run a pipe or wire through the bare bones of a wall (the studs), but much more difficult later when the skin of gypsum board or other material has been applied.

Walls and Ceilings You should have decided long before this moment what material is to be used for wall and ceiling surfaces, but the common options these days are gypsum board (also called drywall and Sheetrock) and wood paneling.

The gypsum board comes in sheets, four feet wide and of various lengths depending upon the dimensions of the walls to be covered. The sheets are applied to the walls with specially designed nails or screws whose heads are recessed just beneath the surface of the gypsum board. When all the sheets are in place, a number of layers of plaster-like paste called joint compound are applied. The joint compound covers the nail or screw holes and, along with strips of tape, the joints between the sheets. Gypsum board ceilings are done in the same way. Most drywall is a dull gray color, but waterproof drywall, which is often required (and always a good idea) in kitchens and baths, is usually a bluish-green color.

In the case of paneling, prefabricated,

veneered sheets are available, as are precut widths of solid boards. With the veneered sheets, the finish has already been applied: it saves time and money, but generally looks like it did, too. You and your architect will have to resolve what gives you the look you want at a price you can afford.

There are other ceiling alternatives as well. Ceiling tiles are a good option for some, while dropped ceilings may be suitable if the job involves remodeling an older home with ceilings that are judged for energy-conserving reasons to be too high. But once again, keep in mind the historical integrity of the building. More often than not, the high ceilings are crucial to the appeal of the room, and lowering them may leave the room with a feeling that something is amiss.

The Finish Work In some ways, the finish work is the hardest part. You look around you at the new walls and ceilings, knowing full well how much work has gone in already and how much is really finished. But in a remodeling job, you are probably only about half done.

Finish work often takes a disproportionately long time. But good finish work can make the space just right; on the other hand, poor finish work can render the whole job a failure.

Still, you shouldn't allow the carpenters and other tradesmen to come and go and finish at a snail's pace while they are working on other people's jobs.

The finish work falls into two basic categories, the mechanical installations and the surface finishes.

MECHANICAL INSTALLATIONS. The plumbers put in your toilet and sink at this stage (it's called "trimming out" or "setting the fixtures"). The electricians will install your dining-room chandelier and your new electric range. The plugs and light switches get tied in now, and the carpenters can remove their extension cords from the part of the house they are not working on, for the power will come on in the remodeled area. The mechanical work must be meticulously coordinated with the surface finish work: the toilet goes on top of the tile floor, so the tile man must do his bit before the plumber can do his.

SURFACE FINISHES. Surface work includes everything from putting down the tile, wood, or carpeting on the floors to hanging the doors and applying the casings around the windows and doors, and moldings at the baseboard and ceiling. Kitchens get their cabinets. Doorknobs get attached. Switch and plug covers are applied. Painting gets done, too, along with a thousand other things.

This is a time when your inspections are most important. You should be available to the workers, but not in their way. Often there are many questions that come up at the last minute, and if they know you are there to answer their questions—or will be at a certain time—you're more likely to get what you want.

On the other hand, if in your visits to the work site you notice that the moldings don't match at one point or that a door doesn't close, don't take it upon yourself to bring up everything with the nearest workman, or even with his boss. Make a list.

This list of corrections is called a "punch list." The punch list isn't a daily gift for your architect or contractor. Give it to him, say, twice a week. Keep a copy for yourself, too, and follow up before you give him the next one to make sure what you asked for got done. If it didn't, find out why.

Coming to Completion After your contractor has completed his job, he should clean up his mess. He shouldn't leave the bathtub with a gritty layer of grout in it, and you should be able to see yourself in the mirror. There also should be no tools or materials tucked away in a corner of your basement or garage.

The Schedule

Since no two houses are the same, it follows that the construction of each differs from the next. Even virtually identical tract houses will require differing schedules, since every site is little different and inclement weather will interfere here when it didn't there.

More expensive houses take longer to build, not least because their greater expense means more materials and more labor, meaning

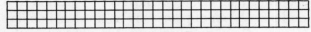

CONSTRUCTION SCHEDULE

Step	Task	Time Required
1	Surveyor staking foundation location	1/2 day
2	Excavation and, if necessary, clearing and tree removal	1–2 days
3	Footing and foundation work, including time for curing concrete, installing drain tile, waterproofing, backfilling, etc.	2–3 weeks
4	Framing	1–3 weeks
5	Roofing and flashing work, chimney installation	1–2 weeks
6	Window, exterior door installation, siding, trim	2–4 weeks
7	Electrical, plumbing, other rough-ins (overlaps with Step 6) and insulation	1–2 weeks
8	Walls and ceilings	2 weeks
9	Finish work: interior trim, doors, floors, cabinets, painting, set fixtures, etc.	4–8 weeks
10	Punch list, final inspection, etc.	1 week

more time. The least expensive houses often take the longest to build because the principal cost saving is usually an absence of skilled, paid-by-the-hour labor. When the owner builds his own home, it can take decades.

When it comes to renovations within a house, the range is even greater. A simple remodeling like, say, the removal of a partition wall and a new coat of paint may be finished in a day or two. On the other hand, I know of one detailed restoration of an elegant and large Second Empire Victorian home near Albany, New York, that has cost more than a million dollars and is in its third year.

These caveats aside, however, the preceding schedule should give you some sense of the time required for various tasks in new construction. If your project involves no new construction, you can still get some sense of the time required by eliminating the steps that don't apply and totaling the remainder.

The Last Word One of the most common problems is the situation where the finished product doesn't meet the needs or expectations of the homeowner. It simply doesn't have to be that way. Craftsmanship may have no satisfactory legal definition (despite its being the single most important aspect of evaluating any workmanship), but it is possible to distinguish quality work from shoddy before the wrong personnel are hired or the last payment is made—in short, before it's too late.

If you are new to the building trades, you are no doubt nervous about how you will know good work from bad. Are you afraid that you will find yourself confronted by tradesmen who, like your auto mechanic, suddenly start speaking words you don't understand and which you're pretty sure don't mean anything at all?

Yes, Virginia, there is a twilight zone, but you really don't have to worry about stumbling into it. The inspection process at a construction site is probably a good deal more familiar to you than you know.

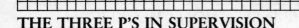

THE THREE P'S IN SUPERVISION

As your renovation or construction project is going on, you will have to deal with the workmen. Even if you feel comfortable with them—and especially if you don't—it is important that you keep a couple of considerations in mind.

THE PROFESSIONALS: These men and women are pros in their own worlds. You need them. You wouldn't dream of buying the parts for a car and assembling it yourself, would you? In the same way that you leave a mechanic to do his job himself, let the carpenters and electricians and plumbers do theirs. Watch if you wish, but don't interfere.

PERSPECTIVE: Step back, count to ten, think before you speak. Speak your mind but with a little perspective. Don't violate chains of command. Yes, you're the boss, but unless you are also acting as your own GC, you are not the only boss.

PATIENCE: Be polite and complimentary. Even if you are not totally satisfied with the work, you are better off finding something good to say about part of it (to the fellow wielding the hammer as well as his boss) and then, through the proper channels, asking for the problem areas to be corrected. It is human nature to want to do better work for someone who appreciates it and, conversely, to be less inclined to work for the person who doesn't know how to do anything but complain.

The key rule is: Use your common sense. Do things look right? Are the walls plumb, the openings square, the horizontal surfaces level?

You don't need to be an expert to supervise construction.

You won't need to master the terminology of each trade.

THE INSPECTION CHECKLIST

THE EXCAVATION AND FOUNDATION

Be on site for the surveyor's work. Check to be sure the house is being located where it is supposed to be.

Either you or your architect should measure the foundation to be sure its dimensions coincide with those on the foundation plan.

ROUGH CONSTRUCTION

Once again, your key concern is to verify that what is being built coincides with what the plans call for. Use your tape to measure the rooms as they take shape. Is each as tall, wide, and broad as it is supposed to be?

When the interior partitions are in place, check the locations and sizes of doors and other openings.

At some point when you won't be interfering with the workers, spend an hour walking through what will be a typical day for you in your new space. From the morning shower and breakfast through your work and recreation schedule, the other meals and entertaining and other activities, try to imagine what it will be like living in the new space. Now is the last chance to correct any unanticipated functional problems in the configuration.

THE MECHANICAL SYSTEMS ROUGH-INS

Check locations of electrical plugs, switches, and light boxes. Is each where the plan says it should be and where you want it?

How about the plumbing fixtures?

Does each room have the specified ventilation, heating, and/or air-conditioning ducts or pipes? (Heating pipes are usually an inch or more in diameter; plumbing pipes are more often about one-half inch.)

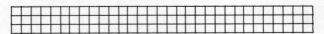

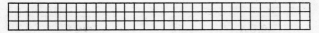

Are the phone lines and alarm systems properly located?

Did you ask for any special requirements (a dedicated electrical line for your computer, an extra plumbing line for that whirlpool you want to buy when you have the spare cash, whatever)? Are the mechanical systems in place for those needs?

THE WALLS AND CEILINGS

Before the painters arrive, check the work done with the joint compound. Is the surface flat and uniform, or can you see the dimples around the nail or screw holes? Can you see the joints between the sheets? How about corners, and if you are not planning on any moldings at the ceiling-wall joint, how do the surfaces look there?

If ceiling tiles, paneling, or wood strips have been applied, are the edges of the pieces parallel? Are they level or plumb? The longer the lines, the more visually insulting they will be to you and your guests' eyes if they veer off up or down or to one side or the other.

THE FINISH WORK

Make your punch list as you inspect. Always carry a small pad or notebook with you—it is critical to write things down. Don't trust to your memory.

Check electrical outlets and switches. Are they straight? Once the power is on, do they work? In particular, check three-way switches: does each control the correct light properly? Check any built-in units: does the heater in the bathroom work? Any wiring trouble is less expensive and time-consuming to fix now before the final coat of paint or wallpaper goes on.

Are the plumbing fixtures located where they are supposed to be? Once the water is on (it'll be

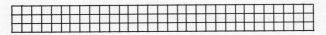

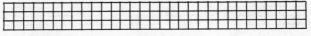

one of the last things to happen, so don't be
concerned if you can't check it until well into
the process), do the drains work and is the hot
water hot?

Check the moldings and other trim pieces. Is the
fit tight and are the cuts even? Are there visible
saw lines or hammer marks? If the wood trim is
to be painted, then careless work is easily
covered with wood filler and the paint that
follows. However, if you are only sealing the
wood, pay special attention to the care with
which it was installed.

Check the doors and windows: do they open,
close, latch, and swing as they should?

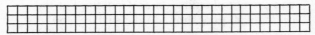

You have allies. If you have an architect
and a GC working with you, regard them as your
Joint Chiefs of Staff. You are still the supreme
(i.e., check-signing) commander, but their advice
is invaluable. You have some outside help, too,
in the municipal inspectors. They may be a pain
to your subs, but a fair and reasonable inspector
will be concerned not so much with dotting the
i's as with safety and quality. If you make sure
your subs understand that their work is to be
done according to code, the inspectors will cost
you nothing even if they make your subs undo
some work already completed. It is the subs'
problem in such instances.

If you are not guided by a GC or an
architect and don't trust your own instincts, you
might consider hiring an inspector or a professional engineer to help. You might arrange for
him to join you on a weekly inspection, or at
three or four different times during the construction to be decided ad hoc.

Make sure you inspect before you write
your check. Be sure you are paying for completed
work and that it's good work.

You don't have to be there every day. Lunch hours, after five o'clock, and occasional visits for emergencies or just to check on progress should suffice. Too much time spent at the site can be inhibiting to the workers. If you have hired well, the pros will know their jobs and want to get on with them. They make their money from completing jobs, not chatting about or explaining them.

7
THE FINAL
PAYMENT

One renovation job I recently watched from start to finish was on a friend's apartment on New York's Upper West Side. Nini was forced to live elsewhere during the months it took to rebuild some of the deteriorated structure and incorporate a few design changes.

At long last, Nini gratefully returned to her apartment. She was thrilled to be home again but knew enough about construction to expect that a few things would require some further attention. But even she was surprised to discover that her bathroom door wouldn't close. Why? The workmen had positioned the toilet bowl in such a way that the door was caught behind it.

Nini put the problem on her punch list. It was an easy fix: a carpenter came and planed a quarter inch off the side of the door and it swung freely by the toilet.

You might as well face the fact that things are not going to be perfect when the workmen walk out your door and go home to prepare their final bills. Every time you find an electrical socket that doesn't work or a window that sticks, add the problem to the list. Don't call the subs or your GC or architect every time a small problem is uncovered, but present your list to the proper party (if you used an architect, it's him; if you hired a GC directly, it's the GC).

This is where the 10 percent of the final bills you held back comes in handy. You've got leverage now, so use it. Your contractor or some of the subs may complain and mumble under their breath, but get the job finished before you pay. The stories of customers who have never been able to get a return phone call—not to mention another visit—from a contractor whose bill has been paid are numerous enough to fill a metropolitan phone book.

Settling Disputes

All right, we tried to anticipate everything. But no one can plan for every contingency.

So here are some ways to deal with the aftermath of a disaster. They do sometimes happen. What do you do if something major goes wrong?

First things first. You ignore the pleas of your GC for partial payment and explain that everybody will get paid when the job is done. If the tradesman who is at fault has the GC on his case as well as you, then the chances are about three times as good that he'll come back and straighten things out. One angry customer is an irritating inconvenience, but an angry contractor who will bad-mouth you to the trade is dangerous to one's professional health.

This doesn't always work, of course. Sometimes there is too little money left unpaid for the contractor(s) to be bothered. It's called cutting your losses. They figure you owe them a thousand dollars, it'll cost two thousand to fix the trouble, so what the heck, why don't we just make ourselves scarce for a while, eh?

If you checked your references thoroughly, this shouldn't happen. Contractors don't usually turn into bad apples overnight. But if it does happen?

Next you check what's in your contract. The contract will be at the beginning of any legal proceeding, so even before your dreams begin featuring Perry Mason's rotund frame, look to your paperwork.

You should have negotiated some leverage there. Payment schedules are the best leverage, but if you find yourself without sufficient monetary leverage, check with your lawyer to see what other options are to be found in the contract. There may be an arbitration clause, for example. In any case, the possible remedies open to you are several.

STATE, COUNTY, AND CITY CONSUMER OFFICES. In many areas, local governmental agencies have been established to help consumers who feel they have been wronged.

Start with your city's agency first. If there isn't one or they cannot be of assistance, try county or state departments of consumer affairs. Often you will find personnel there who know the local laws and business and who may be able to advise you on what your next step should be. If you consult with any such consumer agencies, be sure you have your contracts and other records of payments with you.

SMALL-CLAIMS COURT. Small-claims court is an option if you are unable to get your complaint satisfied in other ways. Usually no lawyer is required, the paperwork is simple, and the results are rapid. Small claims are usually inexpensive to pursue, and you may even be reimbursed for your filing fee if you prevail. Check at your local courthouse for hours and any requirements. You may find the small-claims clerks very helpful in explaining procedures.

Small-claims courts are, as the name suggests, for small claims. If the kitchen window you paid $400 to have installed leaks, small-claims court may well be the right place to pursue your action. On the other hand, if the foundation of your brand-new quarter-million-dollar house is riddled with cracks, talk to your lawyer and get him to pursue it for you.

BETTER BUSINESS BUREAUS. Many municipal Better Business Bureaus have programs for resolving disputes. Call your local bureau and ask. One program in particular will be useful if your problem is with a remodeling project. Called "Remodelcare," this BBB program was begun in cooperation with the National Association of the Remodeling Industry. It is essentially a process of mediation that, if no resolution is reached, leads to arbitration, but the Better Business Bureau charges no fee and it may be a means of reaching a settlement. I know of one instance where an acquaintance used "Remodelcare," and was satisfied with the results. Check the telephone directory for your local Better Business Bureau or write to the national headquarters: Council of Better Business Bureaus, 1515 Wilson Boulevard, Arlington, Virginia 22290, or telephone (703) 276-0100.

Professional societies for electricians, plumbers, and other tradesmen may also have such a service in your area. Check them next. They are associations created to serve their memberships, but most are careful to be fair: they gain nothing in the long term from protecting the irresponsible, incompetent, or shoddy among their members, and at least some of them act as if they know it.

Professional arbiters are also available. Even if your contract does not include an arbitration clause, you may be able to get the contractor with whom you are having your disagreement to agree to an arbitration proceeding to avoid your dragging him into court.

Arbitrations vary a great deal, but in general the idea is to get the parties to present their case to an impartial third party, who will then render a decision. Whether it is binding or not depends on the paperwork (did everybody sign a written agreement up front guaranteeing compliance with the decision of the arbiter?). At the very least it is an opportunity to sit down with a cooler head to try to solve the problem.

If none of these options works, you have two choices. Swallow your pride and get somebody else to fix it or get your lawyer on the case.

Optional Players

When your job nears completion, you may want a couple of other pros to come in and help with the finish. You should, however, arrange for their services well in advance of the last broomful of sawdust being swept up and out.

THE INTERIOR DECORATOR. Your architect may be willing to consult with you on your interior decoration if you wish. He may be able to get you trade discounts, too. If the time involved is simply a matter of a session of "What do you think about this?" and "How do you think this fits with that?" then your architect is likely to regard it as part of his basic services.

However, if you want him to help you find what you want, to explore possibilities for you and with you, you should expect to pay a price. An hourly fee is probably best. Establish beforehand what the rate will be and how many hours the job will probably take.

If you wish to hire a specialist, you have a great variety to choose from. The good ones have great skills at blending colors and textures and can do wonders on limited budgets as well as large ones.

Selecting one is quite like finding an architect, in that you must make a judgment that you can work with the interior decorator, that the decorator's tastes and yours are compatible. There are interior decorators who are in the business to satisfy themselves. That's fine—if your taste coincides with the decorator's. Get a decorator who comes well recommended, whose work you admire, and who seems inclined to listen to what you say.

Decorators are not licensed, but membership in one of the professional organizations like the American Society of Interior Designers (ASID) or the Institute of Business Designers does suggest some level of achievement in the business.

Membership in those organizations requires three or four years of post-secondary education, at least two years' practical experience, and completion of a written and design-problem examination given by the National Council of Interior Design Qualification.

A note on timing: All too often interior designers arrive about the same time as the moving vans, whereas their appearance on the scene should be as early as possible. If you are planning to hire an interior decorator, he or she can be of maximum value to you if consulted before all the decisions are made on finish materials in the house. Most architects are quite willing to work with decorators, as their skills are compatible with one another. The earlier the interior designer is involved, the greater your chances of ending up with a carefully coordinated, coherently planned and decorated home.

THE LANDSCAPE ARCHITECT. The landscape architect can do for your site what the interior decorator does for the interior. He decorates, too, except that the raw materials are bushes and trees and plants. He also has an architectural function in that he may advise you to add a stone wall, to regrade portions of the yard, or to make other topographical changes in its configuration. In that sense, he, too, is concerned with the geometrics of spaces and shapes, just as your architect is.

A fully trained landscape architect will have studied horticulture, art history, and engineering. His or her expertise will extend from which perennials will survive in the shade to the design and placement of retaining walls and drain lines and paved areas.

A landscape architect, like an interior designer, is not a requirement on every job. If your home project involves only the interior, obviously the landscape architect is irrelevant. Even if you are concerned with your yard, your architect or even a local nurseryman may provide you with the guidance and materials you need.

Home, Sweet Home

So here we are. The paint is dry, the toilets flush, the contractor's tools are finally gone. The bills are paid.

This is the good part. By this point you will have made it through lots of sleepless nights, confronted some expenses that astonished you (and been surprised at the reasonableness of some others), and been struck dumb by one or more of the magicians who can take a pile of materials and turn it into a key part of your home.

Have a seat. Relax. Enjoy the feel and comfort of what you have wrought. And promise me something, okay? Don't even think about your next project. For at least a week.

GLOSSARY

ALLOWANCE: The value of an item on the specification sheets; when a substitute material is used, the
portion of its cost that is greater or less than the originally specified material shall be added to or deducted
from the total price.

BEAM: A main horizontal structural member in the
construction of a frame house (cf. POST, JOIST, and
STUD).

BEARING WALL: A wall that carries some or all of
the weight of the structure above.

BUILDING CODES: National, state, and local regulations governing construction materials and tech-
niques in the interests of safety, health, and other
considerations.

BUILDING PAPER: The material, often asphalt-im-
pregnated "tar paper," applied to the sheathing prior
to the application of the finished siding or roof material; also called "felt."

CASING (window and door): The molding used to
trim door and window openings at the jambs.

CHAIR RAIL: An interior molding located at waist
height that is intended to protect wall surfaces.

CHANGE ORDERS: The contractual amendments
specifying material, labor, and/or cost changes from
the original specifications or schedule.

CLOSING: The meeting at which the legal formalities
of a real estate sale are completed, including the
transfer of the deed from the seller to the buyer; also
called "settlement" in some regions.

CONSTRUCTION MANAGER: An architect or
other expert hired to supervise a construction project
for a fee or a fixed percentage of its cost.

CORNICE: The decorative horizontal finish that
projects at the crown of an exterior or interior wall.

COST-PLUS CONTRACT: An agreement in which the homeowner and contractor agree in advance on a percentage of the total construction cost as a fee for the contractor's services (cf. LUMP-SUM CONTRACT).

DETAIL SHEET: A drawing that indicates special features of a house; typically, made-to-order cabinetry requires detail sheets for the builder to follow.

DRAW: A method of payment in which a contractor will be paid on a periodic basis for work completed.

DRYWALL: See GYPSUM BOARD.

EASEMENT: The strip of land inside the boundary of a piece of property that must be left free of construction; easements are usually mandated by local ordinance, often for drainage or utility uses (cf. SET-BACK).

ELEVATION: A drawing indicating how completed interior or exterior walls will look; the point of view is that of an observer looking from a horizontal vantage.

EQUITY: The difference between the value of a property and the owner's total remaining indebtedness.

FENESTRATION: The arrangement of openings (windows and doors) in a building.

FIXED-PRICE CONTRACT: See LUMP-SUM CONTRACT.

FLASHING: Sheet metal (most often copper or aluminum) or other material used in roof and wall construction to protect the joints in a building from being penetrated by water.

FLOOR PLAN: A top-view, sectional drawing that indicates outside walls, interior room configurations, wall openings (windows and doors), and appliance and plumbing fixture locations.

FOOTING: Concrete, usually rectangular in shape, set below grade level, onto which the foundation wall or piers are set; the footing distributes the weight of the building onto undisturbed earth around the foundation.

FOUNDATION PLAN: A top-view drawing that indicates the outside dimensions of the house and the specifications for grading, excavation, and footing and foundation-wall construction.

FRAME CONSTRUCTION: Construction in which the structural parts are wood or depend upon a wood frame for support (as in a brick veneer wall).

FROST LINE: The depth the frost penetrates into the earth in a given location.

GYPSUM BOARD: Finish material for walls or ceilings that consists of a layer of gypsum sandwiched between two layers of paper; also called "drywall" because it is applied dry (unlike plaster, whose finish it resembles); known also under the trademark Sheetrock.

HVAC: Heating, ventilation, and air conditioning.

JAMB: The side or head lining of a door, window, or other opening.

JOINT COMPOUND: The premixed, plaster-like substance applied with a putty knife to cover nail or screw holes and joints between sheets in gypsum board construction; also known as "spackle."

JOIST: One of a series of parallel beams, usually of lumber of nominal two-inch thickness, that support floor or ceiling loads; joists are, in turn, supported by large beams or bearing walls.

KITCHEN TRIANGLE: The design rule regarding the location of the sink, refrigerator, and stove; they are to be arranged into a triangle whose perimeter is not more than twenty-two feet with individual work areas being roughly five to nine feet apart.

KIT HOUSE: A manufactured house with ready-to-assemble components.

LUMP-SUM CONTRACT: An agreement in which the homeowner and contractor agree in advance on a total price for a job; also called a "fixed-price contract" (cf. COST-PLUS CONTRACT).

MASONRY: Brick, concrete, stone, or other materials bonded together with mortar to form walls, piers, buttresses, or other masses.

OUTLINE SPECIFICATIONS: Preliminary listings of materials and instructions to be used for estimating purposes (cf. SPECIFICATIONS).

PICTURE MOLDING: Interior molding located immediately below the ceiling that is used for attaching hooks to hang picture frames.

PLOT PLAN: A top-view drawing that identifies the boundaries and other significant aspects of the land on which the structure is to be built as well as of the structure itself; also called "site plan."

POST: A main vertical structural member in the construction of a frame house (cf. BEAM, JOIST, and STUD).

PUNCH LIST: The list of final problems to be corrected when a construction job is approaching completion.

RAFTER: One of a series of inclined structural members that support the roof, running from the exterior wall to the ridgepole.

RETAINAGE: The payment scheme in which the homeowner retains 10 percent of each interim payment until substantial completion of the job, at which point the withheld monies are released.

RIDGEPOLE or RIDGEBOARD: The horizontal member at the peak of the roof to which the top ends of the rafters attach.

RIGHT-OF-WAY: The legal right of passage over another person's property, usually specified in the deed to that property.

ROUGH-IN: The preliminary stage of electrical or plumbing or HVAC work, at which the wires, pipes, or ducts that will eventually be obscured by finished walls and ceilings are installed.

SECTION: A drawing or model of a part of a building that has been cut vertically or horizontally to reveal the interior or profile; a floor plan is an example of a section, where the cut is made through all the doors and windows so as to best show the construction.

SETBACK: The minimum distance specified by local ordinance that a building must be located (or "set back") from its boundaries (cf. EASEMENT).

SHEATHING: The layer of boards or plywood over the supporting structure of the house but beneath the final siding or roofing material.

SHEETROCK: See GYPSUM BOARD.

SIDING: The finished surface of exterior walls, commonly clapboard or shingles.

SILL: The lowest member of the wood framing of a house; the sill rests on top of the foundation wall.

SITE PLAN: See PLOT PLAN.

SOFFIT: The underside of an overhanging cornice.

SPECIFICATIONS: A series of sheets attendant upon the architect's drawings that specify standards of performance for a job as well as schedules of the materials to be used.

STUD: One of a series of vertical wood or metal structural members, usually (in the case of wood) of nominal two-inch thickness, used as supporting elements in walls or partitions.

SUBFLOOR: The plywood or boards laid over the floor joists on which the finished floor is applied.

SURVEY: The document prepared by a surveyor that delineates the extent and position of a tract of land.

TAKEOFF: A list of materials required for a particular job, usually derived from the spec sheets (see SPECIFICATIONS); used in cost estimating.

UPSET PRICE: The agreed-upon maximum price for a job specified in a cost-plus contract (see COST-PLUS CONTRACT).

VAPOR BARRIER: The layer of plastic or other watertight material applied to the inside of all exterior walls to prevent moisture from the inside from condensing within the walls and to limit air and water infiltration from without.

VARIANCE: An exception granted by local authorities to zoning regulations (cf. ZONING).

ZONING: Local ordinances specifying the restrictions in a given area (or "zone") regarding the use of that land.

FOR FURTHER READING

Ching, Francis D. K., and Dale E. Miller.
Home Renovation.
New York: Van Nostrand Reinhold, 1983.

A book primarily for the do-it-yourselfer. Its clear, step-by-step illustrations can show you how to apply joint compound or build a deck. In addition, however, even for those who don't plan to do the building themselves, the early portions of the book, concerning planning and design, may be very useful in considering options. The discussions of materials are also clear and cogent.

Heldmann, Carl.
Be Your Own House Contractor: How to Save 25% Without Lifting a Hammer.
Pownal, Vt.: Storey Communication, 1981.

This practical how-to book offers specific advice on being your own general contractor. The author, himself a GC, offers reassurance and detailed advice on dealing with subs, suppliers, financing, and other steps. Full of common sense, this book is recommended as a reference for the steps in the process that follows the completion of the plans. One criticism, however, is that the author makes the task of being a GC sound a little easier than it really is.

Home Renovation Associates.
The Home Inspection Handbook.
New York: Doubleday, 1987.

A step-by-step guide to inspecting an existing house. Though intended primarily for the buyer considering purchase, it also offers an introduction to the potential structural, cosmetic, and working-systems problems in a residential structure.

Hotton, Peter.
So You Want to Fix Up an Old House?
Boston: Little, Brown, 1979.

This is a skill book: not how to buy or supervise skills but how to do it yourself. Well written and filled with clear and easy-to-follow illustrations, the book is a very useful reference for the homeowner intent upon performing some or all of the job him/herself.

Kidder, Tracy.
House.
Boston: Houghton Mifflin, 1985.

Kidder makes the process of hiring an architect and contracting company personal. In *House,* you meet the homeowners—the lawyer husband, the psychologist wife, and their children—and the designers and builders. The full drama of the process is played out, from the arguments and frustrations to the satisfactions and pleasures. You'll find yourself taking a rooting interest in this side or that, and learning a great deal about the whole process as it moves from ground breaking to completion. This isn't a how-to book: it's descriptive rather than prescriptive, but a very enjoyable inside look at one house construction project.

McClintock, Mike.
Getting Your Money's Worth from Home Contractors.
New York: Harmony Books, 1982.

A useful reference for buying individual contracting services. If you need specific advice on how to buy such services as air conditioning, landscaping, well digging, and numerous other specialties, this book will be very helpful. It offers general guidance on how to buy home contracting services, but more valuable still is information about what are the standards of professional practice in the individual trades, how to evaluate the work, and how to pursue grievances.

Poppeliers, John C., S. Allen Chambers, Jr., and Nancy B. Schwartz.
What Style Is It?: A Guide to American Architecture.
Washington, D.C.: The Preservation Press, 1983.

Essentially a field guide to identifying American buildings. Style by style, it takes you through American architectural history and, in drawings as well as text, indicates the kinds of shapes, forms, and details characteristic of each architectural style. Its principal drawback is that the houses chosen to illustrate each style tend to be the most elaborate examples and, consequently, sometimes the vernacular styles you are most likely to see on the streets of your town may well be much simpler "country cousins" of the highbrow versions illustrated.

> Stephen, George.
> *Remodeling Old Houses: Without Destroying Their Character.*
> New York: Alfred A. Knopf, 1972.

A thoughtful book by an architect about remodeling existing homes. Its discussion of style and design considerations constitutes an excellent introduction for the novice. It will help you speak the language of the architect, and those dealing with a building of some historical and architectural merit will learn about what the preservationists are concerned with. If theoretical and aesthetic concerns are high on your priority list, this book is highly recommended.

> Time-Life Books Editors.
> *Home Repair and Improvement Series.*
> Alexandria, Va.: Time-Life Books, 1976 ff.

An extensive series of do-it-yourself volumes on single subjects. The books range widely over home repair concerns, sometimes focusing on a narrow area as in the volume *Doors and Windows,* and sometimes covering a wider, more thematic subject, as in *New Living Spaces.* These volumes are designed primarily for those who plan to do the work themselves. They are well illustrated with large, clear, three-color drawings and some four-color photos as well.

> Vila, Bob, with Jane Davison.
> *This Old House: Restoring, Rehabilitating, and Renovating an Older House.*
> Boston: Little, Brown, 1980.

Lavishly illustrated with color photographs and many diagrams and charts, this book is the companion volume to the PBS television series of the same name. It will tell you more than you want to know about the particular renovation undertaken before the cameras, but if the task you are taking on involves renovating or restoring an older home, this book is a useful reference to have on your shelf.

INDEX

Accountant, 117–118, 123
Additions, 17. See *Remodeling* and *Construction*.
Adjustable-rate mortgage, (ARM), 119
A-frame style, 62
American Institute of Architects, 47, 91, 129
American Society of Interior Designers, (ASID), 165–166
Air conditioning: See *HVAC*.
Architect, as construction administrator, 18–19, 53, 86–87, 89; fees and, 9, 11, 51–52, 54–56, 65–66, 113–114; definition of, 47–48; designer/draftsman vs., 57–58; developing plans with, 6–11, 20; finding, 62–64; kit houses and, 61; need for, 49–50; payment schedule and, 53, 54, 56; qualifications of, 57; working with, 65–73. See also *Construction manager* and *Designer/draftsman*.
Architectural drawings: See *Plans*.
Architecture, definition of, 47. See also *Design* and *Style*.
Attorney, real estate, 38, 112, 115–116, 123, 127–128, 163, 165

Bank loan: See *Loans*.
Banker, 115, 116–117
Balloon mortgage, 119
Bathrooms, design considerations, 24. See also *Plumber* and *Construction*.
Bearing wall, 50
Bedrooms, design considerations, 24
Bennett, Richard, 74
Better Business Bureau, 62, 90, 164
Bibliography, 174–177
Bookkeeping, 44, 133–134
Builder: See *General contractor* and *Subcontractors*.
Building codes, 37, 62, 86, 99–100
Building department, 43, 59, 100
Building inspections, 91, 100, 101, 143, 146, 150, 158
Building Institute, 62
Building permits, 43, 74, 99, 100–101